The Modern Survival Retreat

The
Modern
Survival
Retreat

A New and Vital
Approach to Retreat
Theory
and Practice

Ragnar Benson

Paladin Press • Boulder, Colorado

The Modern Survival Retreat:
A New and Vital Approach to Retreat Theory and Practice
by Ragnar Benson

Contents

Warning

Some of the information in this book may be considered illegal in certain jurisdictions. This information encompasses, but is not limited to, such topics as the possession and use of weapons and explosives, self-defense, taxes, and identity documents. It is the reader's responsibility to research and comply with all local, state, and federal laws. *This book is offered for academic study only.*

Preface

"A prudent man forsees evil and hides himself; the simple pass on and are punished."

Proverbs 27:12

Obviously, the image of the rugged, well-prepared, self-reliant survivor sticking both thumbs in the eyes of a despotic invader as proposed in my 1983 book *The Survival Retreat: A Total Plan for Retreat Defense* was not entirely accurate. That book was, in part, about nuclear war, foreign invasion, and the anarchy that's created by those situations. As it turned out, preparing for those eventualities entailed preparing to resist the wrong enemy and to engage in the wrong type of warfare—not an uncommon occurrence given the fact that most armies throughout history have done exactly the same thing.

Management guru Peter Drucker, who has studied such things, points out that the most important measure for a country that would like to win any new war quickly and with minimum casualties would be to immediately shoot their own old, crusty, hidebound, traditional officers. But hold your fire! I am willing and able to revise my analysis.

The last 15 years have dramatically illustrated that the great enemy of self-sufficient people is a government that rigorously and self-righteously demands that its citizens either remain or become mindless dependents. Sad to say, but no government in the world seems willing to tolerate self-sufficient, self-confident citizens, as was true in the formative days of the United States, in spite of the fact that these are the very citizens who contribute most to any society's economic advancement.

Some readers will charge, "You should have known! What, after all, is the Second Amendment about?" Upon superficial observation, it only seems to guarantee the right to keep and bear arms. But historic research undertaken by groups ranging from the National Rifle Association to Jews for the Preservation of Firearms Ownership have conclusively proved that, in the eyes of our country's founders, keeping arms was the same as keeping one's independence from government. They guaranteed our freedom to possess guns so we could shoot back and not become government thralls!

Not all Americans want to remain independent. Life in the cage can be pretty cushy if one does not value the ability to create, travel, achieve, and suffer. This book—and all of those I write—is about and for those who do wish to make their own decisions, who will not accept life as someone's ward.

But assuming a criminally intrusive government is the ultimate enemy and that I fatally erred in '83 is overly simplistic. It's more than that.

Who, for instance, could have predicted the huge loss of basic, day-to-day freedoms in the United States in the ensuing 15 years? Taken completely alone, the tremendous increased burden of bureaucratic rules and regulations has changed the calculus tremendously for those interested in retreating.

To a great extent, we now have a great number of graphic, often tragic, examples, both foreign and domestic, of retreat strategies that don't work. Unfortunately, concepts that do work, which have been tested in places like Beirut, Baghdad, and Brava, are often swept under the rug, so their lessons are not immediately available to survivors. Government officials emphasize only their success in repressing citizens. Doing otherwise would blunt their image as the great caretakers of society.

Although retreaters who *have* succeeded have done so because no one knew about them, future retreaters must understand that it is vitally important that we learn how to nurture public opinion. We must reflect on what we have learned about how we will be treated and how we can effectively portray ourselves to others. On the other hand, we cannot afford to engage in wild fantasies about great conspiracies, the real role of government, or our abilities as survivors.

Like it or not, it is also important to accept the reality that the lure of government guarantees, no matter how phony or impossible, has dramatically thinned our ranks. Accept it— there just ain't as many of us as there once were, willing to put blood, sweat, and tears into retreating successfully.

But also, as is true in my own case, the rest of us have become older and wiser. By 1983 I had seen a tremendous amount of conflict throughout the world, including government measure and countermeasure against those who simply wanted to live free. This led me to believe I had seen most if not all of it. But obviously I hadn't, especially in terms of increased government control of its own citizens.

Several nineteenth-century philosophers referred to people who emerged from hiding after a national emergency as "the remnant." The remnant's role, these philosophers felt, was to provide intellectual horsepower for national reconstruction. My fervent desire, as always when I write, is that there will eventually be enough individuals to start a new, free society formed on the old time-proven model of individual liberty as outlined in the United States Constitution.

To this end, this book is dedicated.

Introduction

Fear of an imminent Armageddon-type event. Run-ins with the IRS, ATF, DEA, EPA, FDA, FHA, UN, or whatever. It doesn't matter. The modern truth with which we must all contend is the fact that government policies are increasingly creating new classes of people who are great candidates for retreats. Stories abound regarding hapless citizens who built birdhouses in the wrong place on their own property, possessed once-legal firearms, or smiled inappropriately at a female co-worker and are now facing hard time and large fines. This morning's paper, for instance, carried the story of a developer who secured all necessary permits to build on his property, only to have the authorities suddenly change the rules. He now faces five years in jail and a million-dollar fine because he flooded marshland to create a pond in his subdivision.

This fellow, like many others, is one of us. He just may not know it yet.

A fine line divides those interested in the field of new identity—especially the international kind—and retreaters. Rather than retreat or drop out, some may elect to change their identity and pull up stakes for greener pastures overseas. For most people, however, retreating within the United States is an easier and more practical solution than acquiring a genuine new ID or becoming a resident of a foreign country, especially when you include the caveat that it be an effective long-term new ID. For purposes of this book, therefore, we define retreaters as citizens who elect to take their immediate families and/or join with like-minded people in going into voluntary, domestic seclusion.

Initially, successful retreaters will have to address some extremely difficult questions. If they don't get the answers right, their success will be limited.

First and foremost is to ask ourselves who exactly *is* the enemy. We must know who we are retreating from before we can understand how to be successful. As a simplistic example, retreating to escape the authorities over a drug offense or alleged financial crime will be much different than for someone who is home schooling her children against government regulations.

From there, we must decide what constitutes a secure retreat against the threat we identify. Obviously, if it is a high-profile situation, governments will bring in whatever it takes to overcome the retreater. So ask yourself if it is a personal goal to violently stick your thumb in Big Brother's eye, or do you simply wish to live quietly in peace and freedom. Your ultimate goal as determined by the answer to this question will play a big part in the ultimate security of your retreat.

Retreaters must figure out what will constitute a sufficient amount of supplies and goods to make it through the tough times. Survival retreats challenge to a huge degree your tolerance to pain as well as your past training in overcoming hardship. I encourage you to honestly evaluate your own situation, experience, and expectations.

For instance, some early acquaintances near the farm where I grew up could stay alive on surprisingly simple food under absolutely abysmal living conditions. As an example, I doubt that very many people would know how to live on a dirt cabin floor, bake on a wood stove, sleep comfortably under a bug net, or use brackish water from a

These retreaters left early enough and with enough supplies to put together a very comfortable retreat.

green pond. Most wouldn't even care to learn. We called it "living like snakes." Is this something you could do?

A big part of a successful modern retreat includes taking advantage of new technology. There are a great many more gadgets and sources of information available today than there were 15 years ago when I wrote *The Survival Retreat*. Terrain and topography, for example, can be evaluated with the help of inexpensive night-vision devices and global positioning systems. Direct solar generation of electrical energy is another example that springs to mind. In 1983, solar power production for a retreat was mostly a pipe dream. Now it's not only possible but increasingly affordable and practical, making it relatively easy to take up life as an obscure hermit and still enjoy some modern conveniences. Other useful advances in technology include the advent of more reliable two-way radios, better thermal insulation, and cheaper, faster water-purifying systems.

But it doesn't have to be all backwoods and beans. Survivors can now realistically plan to retreat in most large cities. Because this is true, we can learn from the example of Anne Frank, the young Jewish girl who almost pulled it off with her family in Nazi-occupied Holland, or from the estimated 1,000 Jewish children who lived hidden within Nazi Germany itself.

Knowing when to retreat, how to get to the retreat, and then how long to occupy it are important considerations. Any discussion of survival retreats needs to consider "trip wire events" that put our prearranged plans in motion.

Finally, knowing when the crisis has passed will be important. Seclusion is fun and interesting to a point, but most of us cannot become recluses for the rest of our lives. Historically it seems to take from two to four years for bad governments to implode and redirect themselves. More autocratic ones seem to redirect with greatest intensity on shorter notice. We should at least understand that we must think about these issues.

By volume's end, readers should have a thorough, fully integrated system for thinking their way into their own retreat situation. You won't agree with all of what's written here. Some ideas may even sound contradictory. It's all a very individual, personal matter, but readers should have at their disposal the benefit of the best *current thinking* and all the good experience in the world on such matters.

Chapter One

Identifying the Enemy

At the time of the Randy Weaver incident at Ruby Ridge, Idaho, when an FBI sniper very professionally blew Vickie Weaver's head off with a .308 round, local news commentators excused this blatant governmental excess with blathering statements such as, "It's all the fault of Idaho law that makes it too easy to home school your kids," and, "If the Weavers had been forced to come to town now and then, they probably wouldn't have come to Idaho in the first place and they wouldn't have been able to maintain such antisocial views." These "views," presumably, are the ones that got 13-year-old son Sammy Weaver and Vickie, his mother, killed by federal agents.

There are many, many lessons to be learned from the Weaver incident. One of them is the demonization of compromised retreaters that always follows officially sanctioned bloodshed. The family, for example, was *not* in mortal danger from state or local truancy police. Until events had run their course, the issue of schooling for the Weaver children was never an issue with the authorities.

As strongly suggested in the introduction, getting certain questions right is vitally important to any successful retreat. Enemies may change, as do on-the-ground conditions, but survivors must always—in the most cold, steely eyed manner—answer the question, "Who *really* is the enemy?" While I

personally do not disagree with many conspiratorially orient-
ed folks among us, I do believe most cannot accurately answer
this fundamental question. Because of this, many place themselves at great risk.

Those prepared to resist or avoid the wrong enemy will
fail miserably. Failure is no fun for survivors. We need to make
the other team fail in their efforts to control us. By so doing,
we have all the fun and they don't.

THE RECLUSE

A passing acquaintance who lives up past the end of our
road in the high mountains is a hard-core recluse. He firmly
believes that there's good evidence to suggest that United
Nations rules and regulations are preempting our own national law. I agree that some examples of UN encroachment exist.
I know personally that, in the areas of firearms ownership,
pesticide use and transport, and explosives transport, use, and
storage, some UN regulations prevail upon us which, at best,
can only be characterized as "curious." But I also know that
the UN has no local enforcement capacity relative to these
issues. Therefore, I don't have to concern myself with blue-
helmeted troops checking out my powder magazine.

Occasionally, in lighter, unguarded moments after we have
spent the day cutting firewood together, this fellow will talk
about his need for full-auto heavy weapons to repel invaders.
But to my way of thinking he would be better served by read-
ing and studying more widely, by making more friends, and
by understanding how the bureaucracy that wants to control
us really works. On the plus side, he is well served by keeping
his head down. It's a form of the ancient Japanese saying that
"nails that stick up are quickly blunted over."

Whatever your perspective on these matters, effective
retreaters must narrow their focus from the broad "they" right
down to specific agencies and officials. They must also know
how these agencies and people have reacted in times past to
situations similar to their own. This is especially true in an era

when governmental agencies do their best work singling out and punishing friendless, inarticulate, poorly read, penniless citizens whom they identify as being stupid and lazy and holding antisocial, uncommon values. These predatory agencies always look for such quick, easy targets upon which they can build "good press." (K. Hawkeye Gross documents this truth wonderfully in his book *Drug Smuggling: The Forbidden Book* when discussing which drug cases federal prosecutors choose to pursue.)

My philosophical soul mate at road's end must live with his personal decisions, some of which—to me—seem very bad. But perhaps he and his little family enjoy seeing outsiders only once a month. Perhaps they thrive on the fact that they are beholden to absolutely no one. And maybe his lack of creature comforts provides a philosophical soothing peculiar to his needs. It's not for me to say. Freedom to do as one feels best will often include the fact that some people will react in ways we cannot predict or that seem very unwise. The truth is that free individuals must live with whatever decision and actions they take, be they good, bad, foolish, or wise as foxes.

THE UNDERGROUND FACTORY

An underground car parts manufacturer in the Los Angeles area produced parts on contract for the big three auto makers. Fred, a friend of mine who works for a shipping company, visited them a few years back in an attempt to secure their freight business. Getting into the factory was quite a number, but his report on what he saw speaks volumes for retreaters.

Enemies of the factory owners were, in this case, the Immigration and Naturalization Service (INS), state and national environmental agencies, unions, competing parts makers, state and federal employment agencies, and other federal agencies. It was more folks with guns than I would have wanted to look out for, but the factory owners seemed content with their role in life, Fred said.

Under the valid assumption that the best place to hide a tree is in a forest, their factory was located amongst many others at the edge of a municipal industrial park. All identifying marks and addresses suggested that corporate headquarters was really in San Paulo, Brazil. Every part actually made in L.A. was stamped "Made in Brazil." All company correspondence was handled through a mail drop in Brazil. At first signs of distress, compatriots in Brazil faxed their American associates with warnings.

This factory, seen as a retreat, enjoyed considerable advantages of production. However, the operators were faced with several daunting problems. Structurally they were forced to produce only a very simple line of steel stampings. Eventually, three scenarios played out:

The factory lost out to an even lower-cost producer.

Their ultra low-tech products became obsolete and fell into disfavor.

Their work force exercised their freedom and decided it really was better and more profitable down on the farm. No company loyalty using sweatshop workers. Employee turnover—always horrendous—could theoretically be 100 percent on any given day.

The lesson here is that these factory people were facing tremendous odds to keep their operation afoot. Yet they cleverly identified their enemy and managed to keep things rolling along profitably with few problems for a number of years.

THE GUN DEALER

A fellow from the Dallas area understandably didn't sign his name when he wrote less than two years ago. His letter explained that he and his associates were in the process of assembling collectors-grade full-auto weapons for resale. He wrote that, because testing was incriminating and noisy and often led to uncontrollable exposure, and because sales spanned the U.S., Canada, and Mexico, they were absolutely paranoid about the BATF. Again, this certainly was not an irrational fear given the zeal with which BATF enforces its turf.

I believe they wanted me to become a customer, but normally I see only limited practical application for full-auto weapons. Yet to hear them tell it, business was good and extremely profitable.

Their retreat, located in a tony, leafy suburb of Dallas, was constructed in a large basement from which several 150-foot, 3-foot-diameter underground corrugate pipes were run. Six feet above, idyllic lawns, sprinklers, trees, and squirrels disguised a firing/testing range for machine guns.

This example again demonstrates a proper identification of the enemy and smart, appropriate countermeasures to avoid detection by them. Recent experience abundantly suggests that, in part because BATF is a large organization with great enforcement responsibility, it can operate with limited conscience.

THE SALESMAN

Other governmental organizations can play very rough. I knew Tom Rudy as a "small-town seed potato pimp," as he called himself. Rudy made a nice living, traveled a bit, and was basically outside most of the year selling seed potatoes to potato farmers.

Suddenly, in 1989, he was accused by the Drug Enforcement Agency of being a cocaine distribution kingpin. It was a ridiculous charge, as anyone who knew him could attest. Rudy lived and worked in a heavily Mormon community and neither smoked nor drank. Later it came out that the regional DEA people were about to lose funding because of a lack of drug busts, so they randomly accused Rudy.

"Confess or we will seize your farm, home, cars, and business," DEA agents told him. "It's a first offense, so we will see that you go to one of the more pleasant penitentiaries."

For a brief time Rudy avoided capture. Then, for the sake of his family, he walked in and faced the trumped-up charges against him. Eventually he served a 4.5 year sentence.

Take what lessons you wish from this account. An obvious one includes the truth that anyone can be arrested and sent to jail if their government decides to do so. Another is that throwing a preconceived retreat plan into gear would have been helpful in his case. But the most relevant to this chapter is that one's enemy may not always be so obvious . . . until it's too late.

THE FARMER

Then there is the sad story of Stephen Strickland of Milton-Freewater, Oregon. Strickland saw his farmland, constituting his life's work and livelihood, being washed downstream by the Walla Walla River. In a desperate attempt to save his home and farm, he applied to both the U.S. Army Corps of Engineers and the Oregon Department of Environmental Quality for help. Big mistake.

Mr. Strickland was not a particularly well-spoken or worldly individual. He had little money and no friends in high places. Just the type of person who cannot intellectually or financially defend himself that bureaucrats love to pounce upon.

Had Strickland elected to realize who the enemy was and avoided that enemy, he probably would not have been forced off his farm and lost all of his savings, home, machinery, and ultimately his independence.

Reportedly, Strickland is currently a ward of the state as a result of building a cement retaining wall to keep the river off his farm. He should have been a retreater, but it took him too long to identify the real enemy! Instead, he operated within their sights, and they pounced.

THE DEVELOPER

James J. Wilson of St. Charles, Maryland, is another excellent example. Wilson, 63, is a multimillion dollar land developer who put together a planned community about 20 miles from Washington, D.C. Part of this development included construction of a 20 acre lake on what the bureaucrats had previously classified as wetlands. Shortly before commencing construction of his ideal development—designed so that politically correct residents could live in harmony with nature—Wilson secured all required state and federal permits. That was in 1968.

By 1990, however, the U.S. Army Corps of Engineers suddenly decided to withdraw approval for work already completed. This included permits for construction of the lake within the development.

Wetlands Gestapo demanded a $1 million bribe/fine/indulgence (take your pick), which Wilson refused to pay. The Gestapo's contention was that he illegally filled wetlands—*with water*. Without an evident retreat plan, Wilson decided to duke it out in court. Again, wrong thing to do.

In general, juries are turned off by successful entrepreneurs who refuse to become wards of the system. Unless he wins on appeal, Wilson faces 21 months in jail and a $1 million personal fine on top of a $3 million corporate fine. Legal costs so far have exceeded $5.7 million!

The lesson? People who deal with powerful, autocratic agencies had best have a retreat strategy in place. Jim Wilson was one of us but didn't know it till it was far too late, if, in fact, he now knows it at all. Five point seven million dollars could have bought a truly fine retreat. It surely didn't get him much justice.

THE HOME SCHOOLER

A home schooler came to me recently asking exactly how government authorities would go about tracking down her and her children. Seems she felt compelled to take her children out of public school and was worried truancy police would come after her. The woman was extremely furtive and fearful, bordering on paranoid, of the local school authorities. She, however, had correctly identified the real enemy and required no further coaching in that area.

A complete chapter will follow explaining how people are

traced, but suffice it to say in this case that she sent a letter to local school officials claiming she and the kids were moving. Government schools are very used to this sort of thing and assume the new school system will send for the kids' records shortly after they enroll.

Our home schooler/retreater moved just 14 miles away to another community, where she and a friend took turns working and teaching. No one ever seriously looked for her and the kids because it was in no one's real interest to do so. She was able to retreat successfully because she understood her identified enemy's mentality. By the time school authorities discover what is going on, if they ever do, her kids will be grown and gone. On the other hand, if the lady had elected to make a big deal out of her resistance to the school system, she would probably have been taken down brutally.

THE TAX EVADER

Even much feared, often loathed Internal Revenue Service agents are mostly paper tigers against those who choose to drop out and hide rather than stand and fight. Off the record, two IRS field agents once admitted that the agency believes that up to 15 percent of Americans are either cheating badly on their taxes or are not even bothering to file. Those who are very, very quiet and smart about it often end up paying no taxes, these agents claim. Public tax protesters, on the other hand, are quickly, decisively, and easily dealt with by the IRS.

Experts aware of the IRS's real structure claim it is relatively easy to fall out of our national tax system as long as you are self-employed. The agency gives the impression that they will track delinquent taxpayers into hell if need be, but don't believe it. A tax retreater successfully living in Las Vegas pointed out that the IRS's recent $4 billion computer blunder is an excellent example of how well the agency, in general, doesn't work.

Those who move out of a community and into a different IRS region who leave no forwarding address, who take no mail in their old name, who work in the underground economy, and/or who use false Social Security numbers can drop completely out of the IRS system. It won't work for high-profile tax avoiders (they need to deploy other, more intense measures such as filing their own death certificates), but it will work for low-profile common retreaters.

In general, the policy of the IRS is to send out a couple of letters to your old address, hoping postal employees will find you, or they will contact the credit bureaus for a locate. But that's it. Reportedly agency budgets are so depleted that they will not even bother to dispatch a field agent for low-priority cases. If they do, it is only to make a superficial investigation.

This is another example where realistic, hard-nosed evaluation of one's tormentors will pay great dividends. Lacking such an evaluation, retreaters might tend to overreact. They may unnecessarily create situations of great personal discomfort such as living in a one-room shack at a place where they have to carry in water for a mile.

THE CITY DWELLERS

Are some retreaters likely to be subject to actions of mindless, faceless bands of anarchist mobs?

Recent experiences in Los Angeles suggest they could be. After the Rodney King riots, we know that some citizens who don't like a rule of law will attempt to recast legal decisions violently. Individual survivors must carefully consider their options if they live in places inhabited by such democracy-prone individuals.

This may be one of the few instances when arming to the gills in an effort to repel marauders might have merit. Some small store owners in the L.A. areas affected by the riots treated their establishments as retreats and made sure they had quick access to arms and ammunition. Reportedly, few buildings defended by owners who shot back were lost to looting or burning. (I know it's beating a dead horse, but obviously they were defending against a howling, leaderless mob of disorganized people, not the IRS, EPA, UN, government school authorities, or Russians with tanks.)

A few concepts are in view here. Store owners who accurately assessed local conditions in their area were able to defend their property successfully. Based on the successful experiences of those fortunate few, more Los Angeles shop owners are thinking their way into a personal retreat scenario. Sales of steel-reinforced storefronts, window bars, shotguns, shells by the case, and even tear gas projectiles are said to be brisk among those rebuilding or rethinking their stay-in-L.A. strategies.

So think not only about the government agency that you deal with most but about potential enemies with which only passing contact is made. Research how *not* to become high profile in the eyes of these people. You also need to determine to what extent and by what methods they will lash out at conduct of which they do not approve.

This, again, is the entire thrust of this chapter. Retreaters must take time *now* to determine exactly who will be the enemy. What assets do they have? How do they usually operate? With what resources and resolve will they pursue you? United Nations directives, for instance, may have an adverse effect on our quality of life, but by what vicinal, day-to-day means can the UN enforce those directives on average citizens? Don't stand around worrying about some overstepping agency or "the government" in general; rather, do some real nuts-and-bolts research.

Each of us is dramatically different. In each and every case, very different techniques may be deployed against very different tormentors. Many of these entail nothing more than dropping out of the system. Just not showing up for government duty is one of the great modern retreat clichés.

Will this work? I believe it can work extremely well *if* we can identify which enemy we are retreating from. Recall that the old Soviet Empire collapsed in 1989 in large part because citizens just stopped paying attention to their tormentors.

Chapter Two

What is a Retreat?

Asking yourself just what *is* a retreat is another of those key decisions vital to the success of modern survival retreats. Those who completely and accurately settle the question are destined to enjoy immeasurably greater odds at succeeding. It's difficult to overemphasize this point.

Retreats can be many different things to different people, but always they must be places of hope and encouragement, not little holes into which we crawl to die. Retreaters should firmly believe that wars can be won by nonconfrontational measures. Remember, those who ultimately survive can have a major impact on history.

"I simply plan to jump in my pickup and start driving around if ever I have to disappear," I am often told. These are well-meaning but horribly inexperienced retreaters talking. Generally they seem to be people who don't want to admit they may have to retreat. They can't face what lies ahead or are really more interested in spending time in front of the TV.

Driving around might work for some resourceful people with new IDs, but it is never a viable retreat strategy. This was true in 1983, and it's even more true today. We have many fresh examples from places like Bosnia, Rwanda, and Burma. Road blocks, bandits, and ambushes are just some of the hazards faced by those who try to retreat on the open road. Other

A retreat can be extremely humble, such as this one.

A Seattle-area retreater determined that his situation would never be so dangerous that he could not use this warehouse as a retreat. It features a relatively nice but small apartment with many amenities.

grave problems include continued exposure to authorities, lack of money and personal possessions, no semblance of comfort, no access to medical help, and many other hassles. This is not retreating.

Furthermore, history is jammed with examples of fleeing citizens who, by reason of war, famine, political upheavals, bureaucratic edicts, or whatever, have been forced to accept life as refugees. These pitiful people have no means of protecting, feeding, cleaning, or healing themselves. All their pride is removed as they become completely dependent on others for absolutely everything. They are herded like cattle from one place to another where they can be kept out of sight, creating minimal political embarrassment for their government. The basic fact remains—*don't ever become a refugee.*

Firmly keep in mind that a retreat is a well-stocked, preplanned hiding place, providing sufficient cover to keep you out of sight and out of mind till the emergency passes, whatever you determine that to be. One more time—a retreat is a place to go and live, not some sort of survivors' dinosaur graveyard where we go to die. Never forget this extremely simple but vital mind-set.

Chapter Three

Picking a Physical Retreat Location

Physical retreat locations must always provide the basic necessities of life. This is a fairly short list—food, water, and shelter—but all must be available absolutely without fail. For people used to turning their taps for water or thermostats for heat, it is tough to overemphasize this point. I cannot evaluate the garden potential of soil around your proposed retreat location. Nor can I evaluate the area for fire threat, water supply, or tactical resistance against forced intrusion. Retreaters must consider all the strong points and weak points on the basis of the questions: who is the real enemy, what forces can they marshal, and how can my retreat location hide me or, if necessary, protect me from same, and most basically, can it sustain me for the duration?

CONSIDER AN URBAN RETREAT

I personally am attracted to rural retreats providing ground for a garden, area for livestock, seclusion from prying eyes, tough fire-resistant construction to withstand nature's vigor, and rugged surrounding terrain that tends to discourage uninvited visitors. But clever retreaters can and do find these qualities in urban locations, even in circumstances of deep, deep retreat. Within the inner city it's possible to grow

Some structures appear to be unlikely retreat locations, but if they provide basic requirements of life, they will work.

some vegetables in plant boxes, parks, or road median strips. My dad raised rabbits on the front porch and pigeons in the attic in the middle of a large German city during the Great War. Water can be carried from park ponds, collected from rainfall, or siphoned from central wells. Under most circumstances, it is necessary to establish a more secretive, secure route in and out of a city retreat, and it is always necessary to store larger quantities of food ahead of the crisis.

It is possible to pick a location within a city that can be bitterly defended from attack, perhaps with greater ease than in the country. Urban retreaters can view built-up areas as a sort of terrain. There are underground workings such as sewers and cellars, ground-level buildings of various strengths and resistances, and upper stories of buildings comprising a sort of high ground that can be taken and held at great cost to attackers, much like hills or mountains. Defenders in places like Beirut and Grozny became very good at manning and defending these types of "terrain."

Successful retreats can be located in amongst faceless city apartment buildings.

Official military publications address the challenges of maneuvering men and equipment within built-up areas. Heavy weapons such as tanks and armored personnel carriers are at great disadvantage in these settings. Sight distance around the vehicle is restricted, while gunfire, either very low or very high, is impossible with many of the weapons these machines carry. One of the lessons military forces are taught is to leave their heavy weapons outside the city, where they provide rapid, controlled supporting fire, and to prepare assault forces to punch right through buildings, creating new, previously unthought-of avenues of access. Paladin Press reprints a revealing U.S. military manual titled *An Infantryman's Guide to Combat in Built-Up Areas.* Those serious about making a statement with their retreat within great cities should secure a copy of this book.

Finally, retreats located in high-transient areas such as state university cities are ideal. Students come and go continually in absolute droves, and nobody pays much attention. It's tough for investigators who may be searching for you to sort out leads in these circumstances.

HIDING A RETREAT

Modern technology greatly expands a retreater's ability to disappear into areas previously thought too hostile and difficult to support life. Desalinization plants, for instance, have come down in price so dramatically that it is now feasible to plan a retreat complete with garden on what had previously had been considered to be a desert island in the middle of the ocean. Increasingly inexpensive solar panels are right now taking the place of diesel generators, avoiding telltale noisy and expensive power generation. Retreaters still need a significant breakthrough in storage battery technology, but this may be along any day now, perhaps by the time this volume is in print. It's a significant issue for serious retreaters.

The point is, depending on which enemy you may face, retreats must be private to extremely private affairs. Home schoolers, for instance, who move across town into a new neighborhood need not be as reclusive about their day-to-day life as those accused of some heinous environmental crime. Tax evaders (not protesters) fall somewhere in the middle. They need to remain private, but generally they do not have to go into deep cover.

City or country, the ability to hide or even camouflage a retreat is important. Depending on the threat level, retreats should blend nicely into their natural surroundings. All signs of life, including working chimneys, gardens, vehicle parks, garages, fresh refuse, connected utility lines, animal pens, rutted roads, wash on the line, tended green lawns and shrubbery, and whatever else must be out of view. Try to secure a site that provides an ability to dig back into a hillside or down into the ground, cover from a forest canopy, or in the case of a city retreat, be completely blocked from view.

Even places a mile or two back off the road generate little suspicion if great pains are taken to make everything look like everything else in the area. Without barrels of fuel, generators, and obvious sandbagged revetments, the place will look like scores of others surrounding it (perhaps vacation cabins or hunting camps). Examples of attacking government forces picking the wrong address are many. Unfortunately, tragedy often results when unthinking citizens believe they have a right to attempt to protect their families from "their" government when these attacks occur.

A conceptual rule of thumb is that it is always easiest to hide a tree in the forest. In many cases, for example, an apartment in a row of 50 similar ones is a good retreat. It looks like all the others, and only those in the retreat know its true nature. Same for a farmhouse out in the country amongst many others. These are retreats because of their owners' prior preparation and by reason of their owners' mind-set.

APPROACHES AND ESCAPES

No retreat is impregnable once authorities identify and target it for destruction. As evidence, consider the fact that even relatively poorly equipped local police commonly reduce suspected crack houses to kindling in short order. Crack house walls are often filled with sand, reinforced cement blocks provide interior barriers, and solid steel doors and window bars impede entrance. But like the castles of early European lords, the only real security are their secret escape routes.

A general rule of thumb is that hardened retreats are only safe when they are difficult to approach and when attackers are unsure whether anyone is actually defending the retreat. Analysts believe that the church at Waco was attacked in part because BATF agents could easily ride right up to the front door hidden in stock trailers pulled by pickup trucks. It was calculated by the ATF to be a cheap, easy victory over folks too weak and inarticulate to defend themselves.

Blowing up access bridges and culverts or establishing barricading structures won't slow attackers unless they are uncertain if retreaters are actually present. In rural areas, this set-off standard is about 30 minutes or more of walking time. In other words, government agents who have to walk 30 minutes carrying gear will spend a great deal more time analyzing a situation before jumping into it. This is probably true in cities if necessary distances can be determined. I don't know what these distances are, however.

Some retreats can be fiendishly difficult to get to. I was at one of these recently. We drove our car into an underground parking area and took an elevator to an upper floor. From there we crossed by steel fire escape stairs into an incredible public housing complex. A hallway within seemed to go on forever. It was littered with filth and refuse like something this farm boy had never seen before. Strange and angry noises welled up from within some of the cubicle apartments we passed.

At hall's end we walked down steel stairs to a small concrete passageway along the side of a huge warehouse. Pressing in a swinging window allowed access to the warehouse interior. Across a dusty, littered space was a humble little custodial quarters. There was water, shelter, and storage space available. This was the fellow's retreat!

Were there easier ways in? Certainly there were. If discovered, the authorities could easily cut the locks off the warehouse doors and/or blow or punch a new hole in the building's cement walls. I wasn't crazy about this retreat because of the high profile necessary to get to it through the housing project. My friend on the other hand thought this would deter others from reaching the retreat.

Being able to get to the retreat under your terms and conditions after the flag definitely goes up is very important. So important that many retreaters apply the Survivors' Rule of Threes to transportation to their retreat. But more on that in another chapter.

Finally, a very fine, often ill-defined line exists between effectively holding off governmental agencies and pissing them off so badly that they immediately murder all retreaters. In these circumstances, only escape to another hidden location will deliver the group from certain death. At the same time, alert government soldiers will do their best to keep retreaters from doing so. Without an opportunity to escape and engage the attackers on ground of their choosing, retreaters always suffer defeat. Recent experiences contending with government tanks, helicopters, and armored personnel carriers is anything but encouraging. Yet retreaters who very quietly keep their heads down and hold out in the face of outside pressure might find that the agency they face may simply lose interest or find more pressing problems to attend to elsewhere.

DEFENSE FROM CASUAL INTRUDERS

Compromise by well-meaning, naive neighbors, friends, and strangers can be a real danger. Only absolute secrecy prevents it. I still vividly recall the time in Africa when, completely by chance, a bunch of bedraggled, half-starved orphan kids turned into our retreat. Food and disease problems alone precluded us from being able to accept them. Everything was eventually handled by my Somali friends, but I do not wish to repeat that experience ever again.

Squatters constitute an almost interminable problem on most foreign real estate, where property rights are even less defined than in the U.S. Once on your property, they are extremely difficult to dislodge, especially using legal means.

Casual up through fairly serious official intruders can be slowed or stopped by use of psychological ploys. Skull-and-crossbones signs denoting the presence of poisonous insecticides work nicely on uninformed average citizens who are paranoid about any pesticides. The only thing worse is fear of radioactive materials. Yellow and purple signs warning of nuclear contamination are a very effective means to keep people away from an area. Signs suggesting that intruders could be subject to asbestos contamination are not as effective as they once were, but they could still work if that's all there is.

Also, don't forget the old reliable "beware of dog" signs. The old ones are still somewhat effective, but newer versions with detailed drawings of vicious pit bulls—today's demon

A collection of bogus warning signs will keep casual intruders away.

dog—are great and can really give an unwanted intruder a good excuse to move along quickly.

A recluse beekeeper I met in Australia kept dozens of active hives around his home. He claimed I was the first one who just walked up to his front door. It's all psychological, but many people are irrational about stinging critters. Yet always remember that with little scams like these, it only takes one who knows to destroy the cover.

ACCESS TO COMMUNICATIONS

Recall that at both Waco and Ruby Ridge, cutting off outside communications to the retreats was a first priority of siege forces, and all subsequent information about the situations was filtered through government spokesmen. Retreaters shouldn't plan to be discovered and made a target, but if it happens, good, unfettered communications with the outside is among the best means of staying alive. If you don't have open communications to an independent audience, government agents can and will kill you and your family, burn the retreat, bulldoze it over, act like nothing ever happened, and claim that they were operating in the best public interest. We didn't know this was important 15 years ago, but time and experience have demonstrated that it has become a life-or-death part of the equation.

Retreat communications, therefore, must be redundant. Although there may be a phone line running into a retreat, it will immediately be taken over by the authorities if the retreat is compromised. Therefore, other possible communications links could be maintained by cell phone, private hidden land line (perhaps several), ham radio, CB radio, internet access, short-range broadcast TV, large message boards or sheets hung from upper windows, secret courier, coded flashing lights, passenger pigeons, rockets with messages, messages in bottles floated downstream, or whatever device or method your fertile and desperate mind can devise. Such alternate communications must be tailored to your retreat's location.

A quick note about the internet. Because the net offers instantaneous communication to a worldwide audience, its potential value as a public relations and survival tool cannot be overemphasized. A well-crafted message or series of messages flashed to reporters, students, like-minded citizens, and open-minded people everywhere can go a long way to addressing the often wild accusations that will be heaped upon you and your group by government spin doctors.

For the seriously computer literate, a digital scanner incorporated into your setup could prove to be a valuable tool. For example, detailed photos could be taken from within a retreat showing any and all evidence of government violence and aggression, scanned into your computer, and sent out over the net to a multiple of sites. Imagine if the Branch Davidians had been able to show to the world photos of bullet holes coming *in* the front door and *through* the roof before government bulldozers demolished the crime scene.

But, you may say, *access to the internet requires a phone line, and that's the first line of communication the authorities will cut.*

True, but the propaganda value of such a predictable act can play into your hands nicely. Consider that dictatorial regimes the world over keep an iron grip on what type of information they allow their citizens to acquire over the internet. If the uniformed representatives of the "land of the free" were to suddenly cut off your messages to the outside world and insist that reporters listen only to their appointed mouthpieces, even the most jaded of government apologists will take note of the implications. This makes it especially important to get out a reasonable, logical, well-written, complete statement *before* your internet access is eliminated.

DEFENSE AGAINST HEAVY WEAPONS

Retreaters who by prior decision decide they will duke it out against a serious government assault can do a few things to improve their situations. But their retreat will eventually be destroyed unless—and this is a very big unless—government forces find they are embroiled in several simultaneous assaults with attending adverse public reaction. Even in very autocratic societies, officials may find public outcry to be so great they must settle the issue peaceably. Before this ever happens, however, we retreaters must become much better at explaining our position and manipulating public opinion.

When preparing to defend against heavy weapons, the entire trick is to place the retreat on terrain over which such equipment has difficulty operating. Most country worldwide is *not* good tank country. Water, rock, steep terrain, and swampy, wet ground all deter heavy machinery. Even dreary, flat Iowa farm ground is impassable to heavy equipment when it is water soaked, which can be up to half the year. Large tanks and APCs stick in mud easily, throw tracks, and cut up trails, explaining in part why armor units always include retriever-type machines carrying large cable winches.

Extremely wise or fortunate retreaters may select a location that lures and channels heavy machinery over preplaced homemade mines, which can tip the machines or cut their treads. In some cases, privately owned Caterpillar-type track-laying machinery can be used to upset or disable attacking equipment. This and related topics will be covered in more detail in Chapter 9.

If the last few years have taught us anything, it is that retreaters only win if they stay invisible. Carefully pick a well-considered location that provides all of the elements necessary for life, some means of resupply, access and egress, uncompromised communications, and shelter from questioning eyes. Creating a tough access situation or hardened perimeter to deter attackers are only poor second lines of defense to keeping out of sight.

Chapter Four

What to Stock
and
Other Considerations

Basic needs of life are not complex.

Usually they are broken down into simple categories of food, water, shelter (including clothes and heat), and an item gurus refer to as "self-actualization." (Self-actualization is whatever keeps you happy and content while life goes on. It may be classified as "quality of life." Obviously it's more important for some than others.) Overall it's not a terribly long list, but retreaters must always recall that without even one of these elements, life ends quickly.

The key is finding seclusion and invisibility relative to dangers actually faced while also providing these most basic needs. As a rule, none of us will be able to duke it out successfully with agents of our government. We may hold out till those agents can no longer endure the embarrassment of the situation, but that's another issue. Historically, private citizens have rarely been able to outgun their governments.

STOCKING A CITY RETREAT

Finding an ideal hidey-hole that provides all our requirements is always tough, city or country. Because I know how to raise a garden, find game, raise livestock for slaughter, develop water supplies, and so forth, I tend to think in terms of

Retreaters should always practice the "Rule of Threes" for essential supplies. This retreat has abundant stored supplies. (See page 40.)

Retreats that provide renewable necessities of life such as this garden are best.

Three female rabbits can provide sufficient protein for a family of four.
They require little food themselves.

Water is one of the few absolutely essential requirements for life. The water in this stale pond won't be tasty, but it will sustain life in an emergency.

country retreating. But country retreating is not necessary or desirable if you have appropriate city skills.

Clever city retreaters can tap in to sources of energy such as a gas main, power line, or in extremely simplistic cases the back of a coal storage bin. They can raise a little food and livestock, otherwise living on stored supplies. Country survivors usually have access to food, water, and energy but must work much harder to develop them.

Because resupply in cities can be tenuous, urban retreaters need to more accurately predict how long they will need to keep out of sight. They must figure out how many barrels of fuel oil, bags of dried peas and lentils, water purification kits, medical supplies, or whatever will last them through the duration.

Jewish teenager Anne Frank is something of an example. Her family went into hiding after the start of the Nazi occupation of Holland. Rather than raising a garden or keeping rabbits or pigeons, their food resupply came from friends and family who furtively ventured out into local markets. Given these conditions, Anne's wealthy father stored money at the retreat rather than huge quantities of food. It was a dangerous strategy that eventually failed.

Neighbors turned in the Frank family and several friends to the Gestapo, probably as a direct result of observing people with quantities of food entering their retreat. It is likely that no one would have been compromised if they had all remained invisible.

HOW MUCH TO STORE?

How much food, clothing, fuel, and clothes should you store at the retreat? A great number of survival books and articles have been written on this subject alone. One interesting evaluation uses as a benchmark records of grubstakes taken out by early miners. Usually it comes down to two things: your present consumption experience and how much money is available for stored supplies. Storage facilities available at the retreat can be a factor as well—constraints placed on Anne Frank's family by very limited storage space, a relatively large number of people in the retreat, and the long retreat duration ultimately took their deadly toll.

As for the basics, retreaters worldwide generally figure for about 1.5 pounds of highly concentrated edibles, a gallon of water, and usually a gallon of fuel per person per day.

Most retreaters can get away with storing relatively small amounts of sturdy, quality clothing, which really doesn't wear out when fashion and first impressions are no longer important. But do not overlook shoes, which are our most common wear item when engaged in hunting, gathering, and gardening. Figure on at least one pair of shoes per person per year unless your retreat is located in very rugged country. Then it may be wise to store two or three pairs of heavy shoes per year as well as boots and repair supplies.

Storing medical supplies and accompanying texts is important. Several reference books, including my recent *Do-it-Yourself Medicine* as well as the *Special Forces Medical Handbook*, *The Merc Manual*, and *Where There Is No Doctor* are available.

Some retreaters do not think about the necessity for adequate storage at their retreats.

Wise retreaters make provisions for medical emergencies. Note the inspection dates on the container lids.

THE SURVIVOR'S RULE OF THREES

Obviously, relying on one source of supply for anything absolutely vital to life invites disaster, so all retreaters must practice the Survivor's Rule of Threes. This rule derives from Russian street wisdom (also practiced by some American Indians) that teaches: "If it is absolutely necessary that your pants stay up, wear a belt, suspenders, and buttons on your shirt." As mentioned previously, retreat needs are very basic and thus vitally important because they are reduced to such simple categories.

For example, all humans need water. Right now the tap supplies it, but a retreater can also plan to collect rainwater, purify pond water, drill wells, or store excess water. For energy needs, retreaters could plan to use firewood, fuel oil, gasoline, LP gas, solar, water, or geothermal power, or anything else they can think of or lay their hands on. For shelter, at my retreat I plan to use the main buildings, a root cellar, the barn, or a tent.

Same is true with food. Be certain your retreat provides opportunities to hunt and gather (even in the city), garden, raise edible livestock, and/or trade with someone. Otherwise, be sure stored supplies of food are extremely bountiful.

To an extent things have been simplified by the advent of dried, frozen, irradiated, freeze-dried, and treated food products. Physical storage of food (and many other items) is quick, easy, and cheap with the availability of plastic pipe from plumbing supply houses, plastic buckets, plastic tarps, and plastic barrels and bins available from local hardware stores at reasonable prices. Some of these materials are available as throwaway junk or surplus.

SELF-ACTUALIZATION ITEMS

Initially, many people tend to concern themselves most with the self-actualization portion of their retreat—that is, those items that will help keep the retreaters happy and con-

Many retreaters make provisions to generate electricity at their retreats so they can use lights and small appliances. Staying on the power grid can seriously compromise deep retreaters.

tent during the duration of their stay. They may store T-bones in the freezer, scotch in the liquor cabinet, classic books on their bed stands, or whatever.

Predicting ahead exactly which of these items you will need is entirely subjective. East African retreaters I have known got their kicks out of making it in places others could not. For them, just being able to pry water, food, and shelter out of an extremely hostile environment was self-actualizing. At the other end of the spectrum, a German couple to whose retreat I paid several visits stocked probably 200 pounds of choice chocolates. Several other retreaters, including the famous Randy Weaver, put Bibles in their retreats.

Again, such quality-of-life supplies are tough to quantify. Many retreaters don't know of their existence till they are in the retreat. While living in Africa, for instance, I had recurring dreams about drinking water from a snow-fed, rocky-bottom, free-running creek. It got so I honestly believed I would never drink fresh, ice cold water again.

This retreater relies on his 1,000-gallon propane tank as one energy source. These tanks can also be coated with roofing compound and buried out of sight.

This fiberglass-coated underground oil tank will last without maintenance for 50 years or more, providing an unseen source of energy for the retreat. Note the firewood in the background—this retreater has many contingency plans.

I once discussed retreating with a fellow whose only "nonessential" needs were for his TV! Supposedly he could have succeeded in keeping out of sight for the duration by having a grand supply of videos, a tape player, and a small generator. When I last saw him, he had his bed, TV, and video player loaded on his truck heading out of town. Other retreaters' requirements for personal enjoyment may be a bit more useful and thus more defensible.

Know that private investigators and skip tracers rely on the fact that most humans are compulsive about some items or activities. They simply must come in for their welfare check, ice cream cone, certain kind of truck polish or toothpaste, magazine, prescription drugs, CDs, books, or whatever. Animal trappers, too, catch extremely elusive critters because they know their targets are creatures of habit. If this sounds like you, and giving up a particular personal habit is not feasible, store lots of whatever it is you crave at the retreat.

CACHING

Some retreaters choose only to store supplies while other more cautious people will both store and cache. Caching is generally viewed as a small-scale emergency plan implemented in recognition of the fact that you won't know exactly when the flag will go up. By caching, retreaters can have on hand enough supplies to live till they get to their better-stocked retreats. It is often done when surrounding events seem random and arbitrary. Caching also works for those who wish to stay in their primary residence till the very last moment possible. Those who need to earn additional money to buy supplies, for instance, can have cached enough warm clothes, a bit of quick food, and some weapons to get them through the transition.

American Indians took a sort of middle ground approach. They cached food-preparation tools in various places about their territory. Part of this involved the lack of portability of tools made mostly of very heavy rock. Often when a hostile

Cache tubes showing both permanent and access ends.

force invaded, they first tried to find and carry off these cached tools in order to deny their use to the Indians.

To work properly, caches must be rugged, well-done devices, built to protect against weather and elements over the long term. Cache contents might include gasoline for the vehicle, flashlights, batteries, basic food supplies, water purification devices, extra clothes, traps, and perhaps cooking utensils. I personally have come 'round to believing that weapons in emergency caches are only valuable in terms of food they can put in the pot. City dwellers may use weapons to force convenience store clerks to provide food and money, but this is sure to incur the wrath of people who will pursue the retreater with bigger, better guns. Having said that, I will admit to keeping two AR-7 folding rifles plus ammo in caches.

Under extreme conditions, some very forbidden items such as military guns, ammunition, radios, money, and certain books may be valuable in a cache. This is more of a strategic cache to keep items declared to be contraband out of official sight. Retreaters living in England, where all guns are banned except in the hands of soldiers and police, may have such extensive caches. (For more detailed information on all aspects of caching, see my book *Modern Weapons Caching* available from Paladin.)

SANITATION

Even in the relatively short run, poor hygiene created by lack of basic sanitation can turn into a serious health problem. In Africa and the Far East, I have observed firsthand the consequences of not paying attention to sanitation. Diseases, lung maladies, skin crud, and much more can quickly run rampant. Hot climates are especially tough in this regard.

A few weeks of confinement with one's own waste can cause serious morale problems for retreaters. Studies have shown that hostages (females in particular) have complained bitterly about filthy, crawly buckets they were forced to use as latrines by their captors. During the Middle Ages it was common for attackers to attempt to either starve or disease out retreat defenders. Because an attacking army had years to wait and because castles were often initially jam packed with defenders, this strategy often worked. The Frank family in their retreat in Holland reacted bitterly to full buckets of waste they could not dispose of while workmen lingered in the adjoining factory. Anne wrote that this was especially oppressive in the summer months. They literally prayed that the diarrhea from which they all chronically suffered would go away. Fog of war along with bureaucratic ass-covering obscures truth, but apparently U.S. law-enforcement officers blew up, stopped up, or otherwise disabled the septic system at the Branch Davidian building in Waco, Texas.

Because it provides a potentially huge vulnerability, many retreaters claim it pays to apply the Survivor's Rule of Threes to sanitation considerations. At least be aware that it's an important issue. Expect governmental authorities, who will also likely read this book, to take advantage of the weak link poor sanitation provides.

Chapter Five

Transportation
and
Trip Wires

Our world is full of tragic examples of otherwise intelligent, hard-working, well-intentioned retreaters who planned good retreats but never were able to make it to them when the flag went up. European Jews in the late 1920s and 1930s, for instance, were not stupid—many of them had contingency plans in the face of Nazi oppression, including moving to retreats. Unfortunately, events moved too quickly and/or they made no emergency plans for transportation to their retreats. For some the press of daily events simply overtook them— day-to-day living decisions obscured the real danger, and millions met their deaths.

I refer to it as the "modified north woods" syndrome based on my observation that many American retreaters claim that if circumstances really get bad, they are going to hide in the woods "up north."

"Where will you go?" I ask. "To the deep woods or mountains someplace," these otherwise well-read, thoughtful folks respond. Questions regarding where they *specifically* will go, how they will get there, and what they will live on are best left unasked. They can't provide detailed answers.

I am not entirely blameless in these matters. Other than having a vague feeling that this I'll-just-go-north-to-the-deep-woods mentality was not workable, I had no firm plan myself . . . until I met Bill Munckin.

Use the Rule of Threes if it is likely you will have to get to your retreat
under emergency conditions. Always plan alternate routes.

Readers of my first retreat book will recall that Bill spent
most of his adult life traveling in and out of really dangerous
places. A helicopter pilot, he was one of the very last Americans out of Saigon on Wednesday, April 30, 1975, the day Vietnam fell to the Communists. He was the only person I met
who preached the virtues of planning at least three separate
evacuation plans when in truly dicey circumstances.

Bill's theory complemented my father's advice for people
traveling in high-risk areas. Dad always said that careful trav-
elers must always carry good maps so that they always know
exactly where they are relative to other, better, safer places,
and they should have from one to two thousand in emergency
cash in a money belt. He worked in Berlin, Vienna, London,
Paris, Madrid, Tel Aviv, and Havana during troubled times
immediately after World War II—but who ever listens to their
"old man"?

TRANSPORTATION CONSIDERATIONS

Munckin also thought every survivor should be at least adequate at operating virtually any kind of motorized vehicle. In his mind these ranged from bulldozers through 707 jets that might be available and required to carry survivors to safety. His concepts are certainly noteworthy when it comes to using whatever is available to get out of Dodge, but I found it equally curious that in '75 Bill simply took a taxi out to Tan-Son-Nhut airport, where he climbed on board a charter Pam Am flight the day Saigon fell!

Because I am only marginally proficient with motorcycles, I violate the rule about knowing how to operate virtually any motorized vehicle when suggesting to readers—which I am about to—that under many circumstances motorcycles are an excellent device for reaching many retreats. In skilled hands motorcycles can negotiate more kinds of difficult terrain than any other vehicle. They can be very fast if speed is needed. They can pack huge loads. Fuel requirements are minimal at times when there may be no time or opportunity to stop for fuel. In many instances it is cheaper and easier to purchase a reliable motorcycle than it is to buy a four-wheel drive rig capable of negotiating difficult terrain.

When approaching and occupying a retreat, stealth is a vitally important issue, principally in the case of deep retreats when its occupation must remain an absolute secret. Modern motorcycles are reasonably quiet, especially if care is given not to rap off the pipes on arrival. They can be hidden at the retreat easily, more so than full-sized cars and pickup trucks.

My original enthusiasm for motorcycles occurred upon learning that Israeli soldiers used them in a few notable instances to defeat enemy tanks! Israeli army volunteers riding Japanese dirt bikes tracked Egyptian tanks separated from their infantry units. Many were able to get up on these tanks with Molotov cocktails. It was an excellent example of low tech decisively defeating high tech.

But admittedly, motorcycles also have their drawbacks.

Under many circumstances, motorcycles make an ideal emergency trans-port vehicle to previously supplied retreats.

They are definite overkill if you are just moving across town or immediately nearby to a new start-over location. Some, especially certain dirt bikes, can be obnoxiously noisy. They can't be used to transport bedroom sets, TVs, or washing machines. Finally, only limited numbers of people can evacu-ate on motorcycles. Should somebody notice six or eight members of the retreat team riding motorcycles, security is certain to be compromised.

(As something of an aside, law enforcement people claim that the first thing residents notice when outsiders arrive at a new location is the women and their dress. If it's wild, exotic, or anything but plain vanilla, special note will be taken. Wise retreaters should see that all women are dressed as neutral as possible. It's not a bad idea for men, either. Cammo pants, black watchcaps, and slung rifles will *definitely* be noticed and reported should queries ever be made about the newcomers. This is *not* the time to make a statement.)

Seasoned motorcycle riders claim that, within reason, weather conditions do not influence riding as much as amateurs like myself would suppose. Still, I personally would be skeptical if it hit the fan on a snowy, bitter cold northern night and an open motorcycle was all there was for transportation.

In all cases, be wary of public transportation where tickets are issued by name. Investigators can locate family groups on the basis of their tickets even if they use aliases. Mass transit choices such as the bus, subway, or some overland trains seem okay, since little but cash is required to ride them. Bus and train routes probably won't run past your front door even at city retreats, but if they do, walk back six or eight blocks to the retreat anyway. If it's a deep retreat, use public transport during rush hours and walk in at night.

An associate perennially on the outs with the environmental Gestapo who has extensively planned his retreat intends to put all of his family on a commercial flight that will take them 2,000 miles completely across country. This is to be a very deep retreat if it is ever implemented. Originally he intended to purchase separate tickets for each retreater anonymously with cash. My contention is that recent airport security procedures make this plan virtually impossible. Also, what is he going to do on the other end, where 50 miles separate airport from retreat? Certainly not rent a taxi or car.

Officials who may want his hind end badly will check every airline and train ticket around the time of his disappearance. Car rental firms will be checked and, of course, every bus to or from the terminal will be canvassed. Some travel agencies will take cash for tickets but will probably also demand picture IDs. Officials may do nothing more exotic than check trailer rental agencies.

I am not sure if this fellow ever solved this problem. He may eventually be forced to drive completely across country in private vehicles. In most cases this *is* the best plan. Advance planning must be made, however, to hide the vehicle once it's at the retreat. In one case, retreaters in western Illinois drove their little pickup truck into an abandoned water-filled rock quarry.

*Numerous new vehicles parked at a retreat can alert neighbors even in a
rural setting.*

Depending on other circumstances, use of the Survivor's
Rule of Threes may be prudent. Perhaps your plans will
include using the family car, motorcycle, mountain bike, or
whatever. Commercial train or airlines may be used only as a
final backup. In my county, several retreaters plan to get to
their places by powerboat, as no roads lead in to their locations. It only happens once every five or six years for a week
or two, but if the reservoir is frozen over they face a three-plus
mile walk should they need to vamoose at the coldest time of
the year.

Be very cautious about the possibility of taking the family
sedan to within a mile or so of the retreat only to discover it
has foundered in deep snow or mud, run out of gas, blown a
tire, or otherwise just given up. All the authorities have to do
once they find the hulk is to run the license plate number
through their computers to know you are hereabouts. Take the
plates away and they run the Vehicle Identification Number
with similar results.

In one notorious case a retreater drove along the interstate until he was about two miles from his retreat. He parked his car on the main road with keys inside and walked over a steep hill to his retreat, believing his vehicle would soon be in Mexico or some local chop shop. But it was not to be. Five days later, state police officers finally ran the numbers, verifying the fact that this fellow, who was not really a very smart retreater, was in the area. They got him later in the week on a tip from a local rancher.

The Rule of Threes should also be applied to routes selected into the retreat. It is amazing how often a bad accident or fire can plug a road or highway at precisely the time of desperate need. Ice, snow, or floods may occur. Bridges may be closed. Prudence suggests, therefore, that deep retreaters or those staying to the last moment pick three distinctly different routes, all of which are not likely to be closed by natural disasters simultaneously, using three different means of transport. This allows for quite a mix and match of options, probably too many for anyone lacking good common street sense.

Some retreaters plan to use detailed maps that all members of the family carry with them. Be extremely cautious that all copies are accounted for at leaving time, however. No sense giving the other team exact directions to the retreat. (It happened in the Old Congo. A family of relatively recent immigrants from Belgium left a detailed map along with family instructions. I saw it several months later when an indigenous soldier who couldn't read asked me what I supposed it to be. As far as I knew, no action was ever taken against the retreaters, but all their personal info was out there, and it could have fallen into the wrong hands.)

For a time during the Marcos era in the Philippines, sales of helicopters to wealthy businessmen were booming. One Bell salesman in Manila claimed he was selling about twenty big $2.5 million 206s per month to worried Filipinos with more money than sense. His figures may have been somewhat inflated, but I always wondered where these people intended to fly to and who would fly their machines. I could readily see

Filipino pilots saying, "Screw the boss, I'm getting my own family out." Hong Kong was too far for these helicopters, and even if they reached the colony, where were these refugees to stay? Some personal retreats could have been tucked away up in the mountains north of Baguio, but I never personally saw them. Perhaps these Filipinos knew more about retreats than I gave them credit for. At least they were serious about planning for the evacuation phase of retreating.

It is always advantageous to have all requirements for life prepositioned at the retreat, but for some people this may not be possible. Possibly their perceived threat level does not warrant the time and expense of renting or purchasing a second set of living quarters that basically remains unused. Or maybe potential theft and pilferage preclude a fully stocked but unguarded retreat. Three possible strategies have worked in these cases.

Retreaters only modestly threatened can move earlier than would normally be required by their circumstances. They can haul all of their new life needs with them, expecting they won't have to keep completely out of sight as did the Frank family in Holland, or they can move in with like-minded friends and relatives.

Uncovering people who see things as you do or who are in similar circumstances is not easy. Finding friends who will assist is tough too. Sometimes relatives will accommodate family members in distress even though the issue is not really "their thing."

The downside to this arrangement involves the fact that people are easily traced through relatives. Claude Dallas, a convicted killer of two Idaho game wardens who escaped from the penitentiary to a retreat, was traced and apprehended as the result of a single call to his family almost 2,000 miles away.

Give some long, hard thought before actually moving in with that great uncle in Seattle who already has a great country place with garden. He may take you and the kids in for the duration, but you may be making government investigators' jobs easy while simultaneously dooming great uncle to some heavy blows from the feds.

Should you decide a relative's place is for you, be prepared to lay in an overgenerous supply of basic goods for yourself as well as the kinfolk. Long-term cooperation often is predicated on financial more than social impacts on your hosts. In other words, hit them in the pocketbook and they will throw you out quicker than if you disagree on religion.

In all cases, be certain that all family members arrive basically on schedule at the retreat, if they do not evacuate as a group. Bringing them along personally has charm, but in really dicey situations larger groups are cumbersome and easy to recognize.

If travel is done in smaller, less-recognizable groups, rehearse all plans and options thoroughly. It isn't a serious problem yet in the U.S. but in other countries, retreaters have been fatally compromised by the fact that they felt compelled to leave a safe retreat to find out why family members failed to arrive. Often these absent family members were already dead. All that happened was that everyone eventually became fatalities, including those who left the safety of their retreat to look around.

TRIP WIRES

When to flee for the retreat is always a tough question. Humans very naturally go into self-denial during crisis situations, claiming "this can't actually be happening to me," or they look for just a few more days to tidy up loose ends. Deciding to leave for the retreat is always a tough call, but it may be virtually as important as establishing a retreat in the first place, especially if the retreat is a low threat level type. As a general rule, most people attempt to stay too long at their primary residence, after which time they or members of their group are already in or close to being in official hands.

It can be a fine line, but serious retreaters must maintain constant vigilance. They must sense when the child protective service agency, for example, has decided you are their next poster child. Never believe *anything* any government agent says about not taking property or moving in a preemptory fashion. Government agents are rewarded for pouncing, not compromise. When arbitrary, capricious official action looks imminent, it's time to stop fighting and to retreat. Hopefully this is self-evident to readers.

Knowing when to depart, then, is only possible for those who . . . you guessed it . . . have a thorough working knowledge of how their specific enemy operates. Ask other people who have had dealings with "your" agency. Read books and legal briefs. Talk to lawyers, professors, and even news reporters.

Some retreaters believe that they can get good information from the internet. Perhaps so, but as a stockbroker once said, "Anybody can put anything they want on the internet. It doesn't have to be true, and information posted often cannot be tracked to its source. When you pay free, you get free quality."

I tend to agree. Lots of internet information seems to be rumor mongering, with a heavy emphasis on grand conspiracies. Cross-check against other sources all intelligence taken off the net if possible.

The trick is to be alert to the activities of all government agencies with whom you are forced to deal, and thoroughly preplan if any possible danger lurks over the horizon. Always keep in mind that it is far, far better to leave a week early than a day late. Have specific trip-wire events in mind. When these occur, don't rationalize—get to your retreat.

Experienced retreaters suggest that whenever an individual or group who's similar to you is singled out for special or high-profile treatment, this should be a certain trip-wire signal to leave for the retreat. In other words, if you suspect you are going to be made an example next, get out of Dodge.

As a final tip, police studies have conclusively demonstrated that people who are evading the law chronically break traffic laws on their way out of town. No one seems to know exactly why. Perhaps deep down inside they really want to be caught, or they're simply nervous about their situation and therefore inattentive to basic traffic laws. You haven't broken any laws—at most it's a violation of some trivial agency regulation—so drive circumspectly.

Like old western gunfighters used to say, "take your time in a hurry" as you slowly, carefully, methodically, and quietly depart for your retreat. Then stay there as planned until circumstances shift in your favor. Places like Iran, Lebanon, and the Philippines demonstrate that governments come and go in cycles. Such cycles often do not favor general freedom, but they eventually will change, and your specific issue may not be a problem under the next regime.

Chapter Six

Finding Like-Minded Retreaters

Many readers who write to me about my book *Survival Retreat* ask, "Where or how do I find like-minded people possessing complementary skills needed to man our retreat?"

Unfortunately, surveying recent retreaters' experiences with this issue is not terribly enlightening. Those who have been exposed and compromised by the authorities are probably not a valid cross section from which to draw conclusions. Successful retreaters, on the other hand, made it principally because they were able to meld into total obscurity within their surroundings. They kept their heads down and avoided becoming high-profile targets at all costs. Securing a mailing list of these folks to which questionnaires can be directed is obviously a very bad joke. We ain't gonna get their addresses, and they won't answer questions if we did.

So finding people with complementary skills necessary to plug holes in a complex, deep retreat strategy is always an issue. None of us is an island. Some of us may have a great many appropriate skills on top of great practical street sense, but no one ever knows it all! Often the more we know, the more we realize we don't know. To make matters worse, we all have widely differing perceived enemies and concerns.

A couple of good retreaters reported that they were able to come to an agreement with a local mechanic and an electrician regarding helping out at a retreat. What initially seemed like a workable plan fell apart, however, when no one could agree on the seriousness of their situation. Part of the group wanted to go to the retreat yesterday while the remainder saw no immediate threat. Their compromise involved the mechanic and electrician quietly working at the retreat part time until their situations also became desperate.

In the case of Ragnar's retreat, I am only a very borderline tractor type mechanic. But the ability to fix things is not the only skill I lack. As a result, I have built up a giant library covering all of the many skill areas in which I am weak and for which somebody will have to be responsible. Books ain't cheap, but like the bumper sticker says, ignorance is far more expensive, especially at a retreat.

TRADITIONAL METHODS

Family, religion, and/or political viewpoint are traditionally the glue that binds conventional retreaters—at least the ones we know about. But it isn't always that easy. Family organizations are at best an advanced form of socialism, and all of us know how well socialism has worked around the world. Yet don't despair: reasonably good evidence indicates that voluntary, family-based socialism does work, at least in a limited regional context. Experience in Russia, China, and most notably Romania suggests that societies that attempt to replace local autonomous family units with government quickly evolve into ineffective, anemic affairs with little ability to control events. Families have proven to be great building blocks, mitigating a built-in bias toward socialism's pervasive problems.

I personally believe that rural agricultural family units are best and strongest, but the jury is still out on that one. Don't forget that many urban Jewish families successfully retreated in Nazi-occupied Europe.

Retreats based on religious convictions are probably okay if you are willing to discount the fact that some of the greatest

Looking among one's church membership can be a good method to locate like-minded retreaters.

retreat failures, both recent and historic, have been religious based. Think of the Jews at Masada and the Branch Davidians at Waco, Texas.

Also, many religious organizations tend to do what is best for a charismatic leader rather than what is best for each individual in the group. Generally we can observe that religious retreat groups often come together because it is a quick and dirty method of qualifying like-minded people with diverse skills but with similar sets of beliefs and values. All that is required for instant admission is to mention that you are a follower of XYZ or whatever.

This is not to say that religious affiliation is not a valid retreat criterion. People lacking a specific ability can do far worse that looking among church membership rosters for fellow retreaters. The emphasis is not as great as it once was, but those in Mormon churches still band together in retreat-like structures. In the southern United States it is often members of Baptist churches who form local political organizations in response to overreaching government bureaucrats. So good examples of success stories within churches are out there.

Wise modern retreaters, however, will not give up all of their personal options when joining a religious retreat group. They also do not absolve themselves of personal responsibility should things within the group not be quite as advertised initially.

In all cases, beware of an intrafamily retreat unless it can be segregated into somewhat isolated family living units. Even in family-oriented societies in Lebanon, intrafamily quarreling was a real problem. Americans are not Arabs; generally two or three families are unable to peaceably live together in severely cramped quarters. Only a very tough, ruthless enemy such as experienced by Jews in Nazi Germany will drive sufficient fear into divergent folks to make them get along for any length of time under such conditions.

ADVERTISING IN SURVIVAL PUBLICATIONS

Some retreaters have advertised in various survival type publications for missing skills within their own group. Results seem about on a par with those advertising for a spouse in the personal sections of newspapers. I haven't heard of this working out very much, but there is always the chance that it might. Other than a few dollars expended on ads and some time spent responding to queries, there is no harm trying if your expectations are not unreasonable. After all, don't expect much if you place an ad in *Shotgun News* for a diesel mechanic when in 60 to 90 days you absolutely have to be safe in the retreat with diesel generator purring along.

DISCOVERING A COMMON ENEMY

I know of retreaters who have discovered companion skills in others by being caught up with them in governmental purges. Within my very small rural community, two such collections of retreaters have evolved. One came to be as a result

Advertising for needed retreat skills can be as futile as advertising for a spouse in the local paper. Given its low cost, however, it may be worth a try.

of alleged child abuse leveled by health and welfare bureaucrats who actually attempted to steal different couples' children from them. In this case a dreaded common enemy drove several very unlikely families together for mutual protection.

In another well-publicized local case, state education bureaucrats started harassing quiet, ordinary parents who were home schooling their children. Rather than either rolling over or resorting to a hard-core retreat, they were a large enough group to band together to fund legal protection and start up a full-fledged private school. Members of the group ranged from a plumber to a logger to a stockbroker, each of whom would never have even talked to the other, much less become friends and allies, without the help of threatening education bureaucrats. But within their six-family group they found a math, English, and Latin instructor. Confronted with a "regular" organized school situation, the authorities were forced to look for other, easier targets.

NETWORKING

Other than resorting to family, church, service clubs, or groups formed by outside coercion and educating one's self in areas of missing skills, about the only other workable device is what businessmen refer to as networking. Networking is a getting-in-the-game tactic wherein people with fears and concerns informally talk about these concerns in hopes they will discover others of like mind. Often it's a case where co-worker X will tell you that his cousin Y is going through the same trauma and you should talk to him. Many retreaters report that, gradually, common ground can be reached and each party agrees to support the other even though their individual situations are not identical. It's happening more and more in our society, much more than government officials wish to admit.

Glib people who can quickly and correctly evaluate people while simultaneously befriending them have a great advantage. They can look in their hunting and shooting clubs, service organizations, chambers of commerce, and at their places of employment for people with skills they lack. Some retreaters even have the ability to meet people in bars, evaluate them, and then recruit them. It isn't something I personally can do, but there are people hereabouts who have pulled it off successfully.

The problem is that our government, with its unlimited budget for snitches and spies, will try to compromise retreaters any way it can. Before baring your soul or saying anything important to a relative stranger, be sure to check on them even as far back as friends and family who may live in another state. In one recent case in which I was involved, the government sent a man to try to document illegal activity within our group. I couldn't get any answers out of him regarding his history or family, so I just strung him along for a couple of years until it became obvious he was a government snitch. After that he quickly dropped out of the picture, moved away, and no doubt changed his name. Moral to the story? If you can't check and verify, give the situation a great deal of time. It will usually self-correct.

In a happier, more positive context, I recently networked a contact into something positive for my retreat. Some nice folks and their kids stopped by to talk about my rabbits. It turned out they were interested in learning how to raise rabbits as an emergency food supply. We didn't get round to discussing retreats for quite a while. It was only after I mentioned that I intended to use rabbit meat when other supplies were unavailable that this family finally admitted they shared similar intentions. We both confessed that we seldom talked about survival or retreating with "average" citizens because self-reliant folks such as ourselves have been so demonized by government propagandists.

Successful networking takes incredible preplanning, patience, and luck. Don't expect to put anything workable together within six to eight months of dire need. A year or two is probably more realistic. But keep in mind that it is amazing how lucky people who work very hard can be.

• • • •

I wish I had more to offer in this area of retreat thought. My best suggestion is to get into a retreat-thinking mode very early in the game so you can recognize and possibly recruit like-minded and useful people as you meet them. This way, when the chips are down your ducks will already be in a row.

Any readers with current experience involving finding needed skills for a retreat group, please contact me in care of the publisher.

Chapter Seven

How They Find You

In today's society it is virtually impossible to disappear completely. I have often boasted that I can find anyone, any-where—so long as you are paying expenses. So far no one has proved me wrong. These skills are not particularly exotic or difficult to deploy. Because they rely on such basic informa-tion, even relatively unskilled investigators can find people, especially ones who take no precautions to cover their tracks.

What follows is a brief overview of skip tracing techniques used by private and government snoopers. None of this is profound. Rather they are quick, dirty methods of finding people. As mentioned, this stuff always seems to work.

Two dynamics come into play here. First, few humans can really disappear if funds allocated for their pursuit are virtu-ally unlimited. In many regards, governments are the source of unlimited funds with which to track people with whom they are upset. I once talked to a man who spent 30 years try-ing to track down Martin Bormann, the old Nazi party secre-tary. Our government paid the entire bill, which probably totaled hundreds of thousands of dollars.

The second dynamic is that clever retreaters can arrange things so that the game is not worth the candle, even for gov-ernment pursuers with deep pockets. Should you have tens of millions of dollars that you are packing off to your retreat and simultaneously are involved in a high-profile situation, they will probably make you a target . . . and good luck escaping then! On the other hand, retreaters who keep their assets scattered around the world and studiously avoid becoming high profile have a great chance of disappearing.

Raul Salinas, brother of Carlos Salinas, the recent president of Mexico, is a good example of someone who at least had the financial side down. Although Raul took millions in drug bribe money and was tied to heinous crimes within his own country, he is still out there someplace enjoying life (probably in Cuba). Only a few low-level government officials around him have been prosecuted, mostly for money laundering. They were probably caught because they were not well enough off to stash funds in various places around the world.

But how do investigators find people? Quite simply, as we will see. Other than having access to certain records that are difficult (but not impossible) for private investigators get at, techniques used by government investigators are similar to those used by every PI.

First and easiest, investigators always go to the local post office to look for a forwarding order. Competent retreaters ain't gonna fill out these forms, but it is astounding how often people actually do tell the world where to find them in this manner. This includes those who sincerely believe they are sneaking off to a real retreat someplace or another.

As a general rule, even IRS investigators do nothing more exotic than inquiring of mail forwarding orders at your old post office. Unless your case involves lots of principal or lots of money, the IRS has too many cases in front of it to expend more time and energy looking for you than this brief, cursory investigation.

U.S. mail information is supposedly not available to private citizens who make inquiry, but nongovernmental investigators have a number of methods to circumvent these restrictions. The easiest is to claim the person for whom a search is being made had a business from which you purchased a faulty product. Then postal authorities are obligated to provide not only information but active assistance in such cases of commercial enterprise.

Investigators have access to some fairly vast data banks not commonly available to regular citizens. Some of these are costly and inefficient to mine *unless* users are in the full-time business of locating people. One such company, MetroMail, located in Lombard, Illinois, is an exception. They work something like the infamous pay-per-minute sex-talk lines. For about $3 per minute charged to your phone bill, they will search through about 150 million names in their file. You will get a street address, phone number, city, and state. It helps to have either a unique name or a complete middle name, or be prepared to go through dozens of John W. Smiths until you find yours.

Most of MetroMail's locates are based on post office change-of-address cards, telephone and cable TV hookups, and new utility service orders. Simply installing a phone in your old name at a new location will immediately place you in MetroMail's vast data bank. Their records also track how long you have lived at your present location and general financial status of those living in the same area. The same sources of information are cataloged and mined by most of the other major data bank outlets too.

Many of the same avenues are open to credit bureaus who must locate people who leave town, but generally they tend to rely on financial data—you take out a bank loan or mortgage at your new location and the credit bureau has a locate. Same with continuing time payments on a truck, car, tractor, or boat.

Some pay-per-use data banks have information on car registrations and real property purchases. Transfer a vehicle title to a new state and even lazy investigators have you. Use a completely new fictitious name and you're probably home free. But remember, investigators are on to using the name of your horse, dog, or kids and will set their computers to search for those names. Also, be aware that an investigator's interest will be focused on regions where family friends and relatives already live.

Investigators can find people on the basis of their occupations. I once tracked an expert heating duct man 2,000 miles from California to Kentucky by calling furnace and cooling shops in Kentucky. It only took about three hours and $15 worth of phone charges. I called Kentucky because he grew up there.

"Hello," sez I, "this is Ragnar Benson with the Farmers' Alliance Insurance Company. We have an insurance payment for a considerable sum of money for a fellow by the name of John Doe. He is about 35 years old, brown hair, 160 pounds, about 5'10". Mr. Doe is an expert sheet metal man. Have you hired anybody like this lately? Have him call collect if you think you have him."

Investigators always look for clues in old phone bills. Chances are good you called someone at or near your new retreat within the last year. Usually it's relatively easy, for instance, to find women who slip out with kids in violation of court orders because they often call ahead to their new location for motel or apartment rental arrangements.

Those who have already compromised their retreat by calling ahead can either find a new location or obscure their ultimate destination by making hundreds of random calls to banks, motels, and whatever in many different parts of the country. Otherwise, always use prepaid telephone cards to call anyone in the retreat area. Even better, call from a pay phone on a street far from your home using a prepaid card.

When retreat time draws near, have your old phone and utilities canceled as early as possible. The longer they are out of service, the tougher it will be to track you through them. In an investigator's eyes, such information grows stale very quickly. Living with a small, portable generator and without a phone for a month or two may be a pain, but no more so than being quickly caught at your new retreat.

Also, watch those old credit card statements closely. I have located some very clever people who skipped out with company cash, the boss's wife, or in one case some expensive farm equipment by simply researching old credit card statements. In one notoriously easy case, a woman bought plane tickets to

Some deep retreaters use foreign banks and credit cards to throw investigators completely off their tracks.

her new location and clothes near where she was staying and even paid apartment rental with the card. It was a no-brainer.

Same goes for the checking account. It will be scrutinized along with everything else. All investigators know that checking account information is held by banks on microfilm for several years. Retreaters who put their place together paying by check even five years back are still at great risk *if* their situation is of sufficiently high profile.

Wise retreaters must think through whatever payment plan they intend to use and be sure it is not easily tracked to their retreat doorstep. Fortunately there are still many ways of paying secretly for goods and services connected to a retreat. Effective strategies can include dealing only in cash and cashiers checks, banking in Mexico or Canada, doing barter exchanges, using gold coins or credit cards issued by a foreign bank, and even to a limited extent using money orders. Covering all of these strategies could easily comprise a book in itself.

Certainly the best device for those who suddenly find they must retreat is to file a bogus death certificate. Properly done, a phony death certificate will cut all ties to bank accounts, credit cards, real property, or whatever. Filing a death certificate is not tough, but it is very structured. See my book *Acquiring New ID* for exact details.

National computer data banks keep track of virtually all recorded real property transactions in the United States. Access to most of these is sufficiently pricey to scare off casual lookers, but increasingly they are being made available for a few dollars per minute of research time. It is no longer necessary for investigators to purchase the whole package, which may come on a computer CD that requires costly twice-monthly updates.

It always amazes me that so much is made of ex-spouses who illegally skip out with school-age kids. People of this sort are very, very easily found. In fact, I have come to believe that a disinformation campaign of some sort must be in operation. Government entities make loud noises about these disappearances when the easiest thing in the world is to go down to the kids' old school to see where their records were transferred. Nothing very mysterious about this!

Skips who home school their kids are tougher, but usually a single spouse can't afford to home school. Eventually records will be requested—government schools simply will not allow new third or fourth grade children into their systems without them. Going without records is a condition no good bureaucrat can tolerate without breaking into hives, hemorrhoids, or herpes.

One woman tried to get around this by claiming she previously home schooled her kids and that no government school records existed. An alert, suspicious teacher quizzed the kids closely. In a day or two she had the entire retreat plan.

As a last resort, investigators can run a tap on the phone of a skip's relative. It may take two or three months, but invariably the missing family member is found. In one case I called the mother with the news that I had a large insurance check

INDIANA STATE DEPARTMENT OF HEALTH
CERTIFICATE OF DEATH

Local No. ....   State No. ....

*Filing a bogus death certificate is relatively easy and will throw off
many investigators.*

for her runaway daughter. She was on the phone to her daughter five minutes after we hung up and we had them.

In another case I explained to the mom that it was a large cashier's check and that if I heard nothing by 3:00 P.M. I would have to put the money back in the bank. Because of the expense, mom's phone was not tapped, but the hiding daughter called us personally within minutes. We had her locate from our Caller ID.

One woman was hiding in the same city in which I was working. She actually came down to my temporary office in search of the promised money and we nabbed her. No expensive, risky phone taps using this ploy.

Really determined government investigators will run through new magazine subscriptions, political party memberships, and club rosters likely to be of interest to skips. Those who like to read cockfighting magazines or who are affiliated with an obscure religious sect had best find other interests or they will be found quickly.

People with peculiar medical maladies are often tracked via their medical records, and even those securing routine medical service can be tracked using those records. Anyone who has the Social Security number, date of birth, and full name of a targeted citizen can, for $8, secure "their own" medical records from the Medical Information Bureau in Boston, Massachusetts. After all, nobody knows who you are over the phone if you have the correct identifying info. Once the records are in hand, it is easy to contact the last treating physician and use a pretext to get a locate. Deep retreaters, therefore, must plan to handle their own medical care.

All of this says little to nothing about obvious tracking methods such as securing new state driver's license applications, applying for occupational licenses or permits, acquiring hunting or fishing licenses, or making any contact with any authorities in any capacity, no matter how trivial or mundane. All of these contacts can easily lead right back to the retreat.

By now, retreaters who have not taken the time or energy to look at things from an investigator's point of view realize that disappearing requires well-thought-through advance preparation. Don't trust to luck or circumstances. Do your homework and remove the easy tracks everyone leaves before you think about disappearing. It is better to overestimate the enemy's will and resources than to underestimate them.

Chapter Eight

What to Expect from Your Government When It Goes Hard Core Against You

So say by some twist of fate or personal indiscretion you have become a target of the government. What now?

We have learned many lessons from recent government action against its own citizens. This list is long, at times grim, and not entirely logical. This chapter will describe some of the things you, the cornered retreater, can expect to face when the government turns its considerable might and fury against you.

YOU ARE ON YOUR OWN

During the Randy Weaver takedown, a number of residents of Idaho, Washington, and Montana reportedly contemplated pulling on their cammies, grabbing their rifles and ammo, and heading out into the bush to hunt federal assassins. These were largely old guys with established careers and families. They were not volatile kids going out into the forest on some sort of lark, the consequences of which they really didn't understand. Perhaps the feds sensed that things were heating to a blowup point and decided to end the affair quickly by forever silencing Weaver.

The point is that no one actually came to beleaguered Randy Weaver's assistance in the end. Most honest citizens throughout the world have a tough enough time just feeding their own families. They don't have time to support some sort of guerrilla action out in the mountains against their own government, even if it's very bad. So don't expect anyone to come with assistance when you are surrounded and cut off by government forces.

Several sophisticated studies have been done attempting to determine exactly when the lines on the graph cross and freedom-loving people actually take up arms against their own despotic government. Stalin and Mao Tse Tung were very interested in both promulgating revolution and in staying in power once revolution swept them into office. Both concluded that A) it takes the support of but 6 percent of the population to organize a successful revolution, and B) revolutions always start in the countryside.

But beyond these basic findings, results of most studies are not encouraging. Freedom, they conclude, does not really have a paid constituency. In other words, things have to get awfully bad down on the farm before average citizens will risk everything for something as abstract as freedom. In contrast, socialism definitely has a constituency. You support the controlling party and they reward you with a barrel of pork, backing for your particular moral crusade, or maybe even an easy, high-paying government job allowing you to make important life decisions for other citizens.

In part, this is why no credible advocate came to Weaver's defense and why retreaters today should expect absolutely no outside aid either. Start by not kidding yourself. Should your retreat be compromised and you and your family made public targets, no one is going to forsake all and go to war on your behalf. The individual risks compared to rewards are far too great.

HOW THEY PICK TARGETS

I can't prove it, but despotic officials seem to take a long, hard look at potential targets before acting. Seemingly, a conscious decision is made to harass only those with perceived character defects. Antisocial loners make the list. The reasoning seems to run that only folks who can't fight back effectively make good examples for other Americans who may be similarly inclined to defy the government. The ultimate message is that no one but hopelessly ignorant, uneducated, uninformed, traitorous citizens would ever defy their government. Worldwide, government officials always assume they "know what is best for you" and habitually attempt to demonize and squelch those who think otherwise.

THE SIEGE BEGINS

Potential retreaters who have not studied modern government siege techniques must do so quickly. Understanding how they will isolate you, investigate you, talk to you, portray you, and ultimately attack you is obviously of utmost importance to your effort.

At the first sign of a standoff, a trained team of crisis response people will be assembled. An "incident" response officer will be assigned to see your situation through to the end. His team will include electronics specialists charged with getting wires and cameras into your retreat, life support people who handle sleeping and eating arrangements, public relations people required to explain things to the media, and investigators who will look up police, IRS, school, bank, and all other relevant records as well as interview friends, family, neighbors, and acquaintances. Every piece of available information about you will be gathered and put to use.

As a first step, these government agents will attempt to disconnect or short circuit all outside communications to your retreat. It's a first priority to make compromised retreaters completely dependent on their captors for all outside news and information. (In part, it's why the BBC went to such trouble and expense to keep occupied countries informed of events in their own language during World War II. The Axis powers would not allow anything but their own spin on events to be broadcast.)

Second, the electronic specialists will infiltrate tiny con-

cealed microphones and TV cameras into the retreat. Once
these are operational, the government will know every spoken
word, movement, and plan of those therein. It's tough to virtually impossible to prevent skilled electronics people from getting their remote mics and cameras into the retreat once that is
their goal. About all that's left after being discovered, surrounded, and cut off is to work under the assumption that
everything you do and say is being monitored and recorded.
(Under these circumstances, it is especially difficult to believe
our government's pleas of innocence relative to the burning
deaths of the children at Waco.)

YOU WILL BE DEMONIZED

Always, if compromised retreat situations stalemate past a few days, public relations experts will be sent in whose only job is to put their own spin on things by demonizing the retreaters. Retreaters will be labeled as bad, even evil people simply because they refuse to submit to "their" government.

Whenever it goes that far, every retreat shelter, no matter how simple or humble, will be described as a hardened "bunker" or "compound." Randy Weaver's crude plywood shack was referred to as a bunker over and over again by the Marshal's Service, ATF, and FBI. The Branch Davidian's church and living quarters were collectively known as "the compound" from the very beginning. Unfortunately, journalists usually cooperate by swallowing this fiction whole. They report the official line without doing much independent inquiry, even if it's obviously a breezy slab-side shack out there in front of them.

Other examples of this phenomenon abound. A multimillionaire once started construction on a new home along the shores of Lake Michigan in the state of Michigan. Unlike many of his social class, he was often seen in public. Dinner guests visited his home regularly. Still, popular envy with which every successful person must contend ran roughshod through his community.

The man collected old, noteworthy, limited-edition Bibles as a hobby. His Bible collection, accumulated over many years, may have been worth millions of dollars. Because the collection was priceless and mostly irreplaceable, he specified that a secure climate-controlled display area be built into the basement of his new home.

Once turned over to architects, however, this room evolved into a reinforced cement, vault-like structure. Somehow the media latched onto the room as being an intense threat to local, state, and national authority. An immediate assumption was made that, because the fellow liked old Bibles, he must be some kind of antisocial religious nut. For several days he was actively equated with David Koresh. Local citizens intoned darkly that he was a menace to their community.

Soon, headlines in Chicago and Detroit newspapers screamed about the eccentric rebellious millionaire who threatened local citizens because he was building this formidable structure on Lake Michigan. TV news joined the feeding frenzy, running frequent updates regarding the "bunker." Many of us who saw events unfolding expected to see federal agents riding up on the construction site in armored vehicles with guns blazing. As a precaution, the fellow sent his wife and kids out of the country.

For a time it looked as though federal marshals intended to swoop in and confiscate the man's private property. Eventually, however, the story lost its frenzied energy, and the media turned to other sensational issues.

Moral? It's another proof that those of us who decide to retreat, even if it's not really a retreat, are going to be labeled as bad or even evil if the wrong people find out what we are doing. We are dealing with people who, having no valid arguments and few hard facts, must resort to branding and demonization.

It gets worse. Retreaters with small children at the retreat may be labeled as hard-core child molesters or perverts. They will be accused in most vicious terms of holding their own children as hostages. Officials will also paint the retreat as being a hotbed for all kinds of illegal activity, from gun running to drug dealing. Any past legal indiscretions will be trotted out as examples of the vile character of the occupants. All compromised retreaters will be painted as habitual lawbreakers even if the worst item on record is a parking ticket.

Government agents will always scream "illegal drugs" at the first sign they are facing retreaters who do not immediately throw up their hands and surrender. By so doing, they allow cooperating judges to set aside the Posse Comitatus Act and sanction sending in military troops with their heavy equipment. (That's why there were tanks, armored personnel carriers, and helicopters at Waco.) It does not matter if subsequent inquiry demonstrates that the most potent drugs present were bottles of aspirin.

Two countermeasures come into view here that may help you fight back against the government's propaganda machine. Both have been tried, and both work.

First, it is helpful, to monitor newscasts containing official government statements relative to your situation and do everything possible to dispel this propaganda barrage. Acting like just another average citizen on which the government has arbitrarily decided to pounce is a good start. *This could easily be you*, retreaters must repeat over and over to anyone who will listen.

Second, as Martin Luther King found when cotton-brained southern sheriffs put him in their jails, a short, intense visit to the slammer can provide a great boost to the cause. This is true if (and this is a very big if) you simultaneously have a vocal, articulate spokesman on the outside who can rile up public opinion in your favor while you, the main man, sit in jail. But remember: they win if they can jail you for a long period of time. People in the slammer are in complete limbo, and in our culture it only takes about 30 days of no news for you to become a complete nonperson. To be effective, any jail time must be short.

It also works nicely to have a series of friends, colleagues, acquaintances, and club members who, on being alerted, will make an incredible stink. This is why government agents seldom attack main-line churches or long-established service clubs. There would be a huge public furor over such highhanded actions.

Unfortunately, our side is peopled by a bunch of standalone, rugged individuals. Few of us belong to a church group, country club, shooting club, motor club, social club, or any other collection of citizens who would scream their heads off about ill treatment of their associates. In some cases, then, it's helpful to have an extended family who can howl on your behalf. In the same regard it seems to work to be a well-known socializer who has friends in every store, restaurant, and gas station in town. Prior good name recognition among the community can only help in a bad situation.

So the question here is, how many retreat situations can our government handle simultaneously? No one knows for sure. Probably two might be too many if there is a lot of publicity. Certainly three, if they are covered on the nightly news, is way too many. Public opinion, sluggish at first, would start to turn, especially if there were blood and fatalities. Serious questions would be raised *if* retreat defenders effectively and articulately communicated their message with the outside world.

It bears repeating here: without excellent—not merely good—wide-ranging communications with the world outside the retreat, retreaters are completely at the mercy of surrounding government forces. This is one of the great lessons we have learned the hard way during the last few years. Once a retreat is compromised, successful resistance will probably not come from heavy weapons, mines, and explosives but from clear, effective communication of a legitimate message to the outside world while government tanks and APCs threaten and growl on the perimeter.

Don't ever waste precious communications time/contact attempting to propagandize outside listeners. Average citizens are not going to be as impressed by the fact that you are a victim of some grand international conspiracy as they will be knowing it's their own sons and daughters in the uniformed services who are participating in some sort of inhuman atrocity. Deny the many charges that will be laid against you, and demonstrate that the government has no evidence of your being involved in the criminal activities they allege. Stick to a basic humanitarian message. You might maintain that the government has confiscated all your property, including all your ability to work for a living, using an arcane, foolish rule. "We are not harming anyone," you could say. "We just came here to be left alone. Why has our government become such a paranoid bully?" It won't sell with the feds, but it may help out in the court of public opinion. So ask such pointed questions over and over again until those on the outside begin to ask questions of their own.

Should a retreat be compromised, cut off, and surrounded, unencumbered communications with the outside world may be your best chance for survival.

THE "NEGOTIATIONS"

Once cut off and surrounded, retreaters will be forced to deal with some very able, highly trained professional negotiators. *Always* keep in mind that it is virtually impossible for amateurs to contend with these people. Trained terrorists may have the skills, but common citizens like you or me are at a great disadvantage, even if we take great care to study all available literature on hostage negotiations. We will be under great stress; they more or less view what's going down as a great adventure.

A brief overview of negotiations follows, allowing readers to know in general what to expect. But chances are slim to nonexistent that you, the cornered retreater, could ever prevail against these pros. Don't even attempt to deal with them.

After they believe all other communications are cut off and you are cornered, negotiations will be handled by a senior, perhaps retired, street cop. This guy will have great street sense and tremendous people skills. In all likelihood he will have received extensive training in negotiations at the U.S. Army's military police school at Fort McClellan, Alabama.

At first this expert will try to establish some lines of identification, rapport, and confidence by keeping you on the phone, continually asking you to explain things in great detail. He will ask over and over, "Do you know how upset you sound?" He may ask if you are hungry or want something. If the answer is yes, expect a convoluted discussion about what you want. "So, you want some hamburgers. Is that with pickles, lettuce, and onions? Do you want mustard or catsup on them?" He will use a technique called "nondirect counseling" in which he repeats everything that you have said back to you. Most people take the bait and prattle on for hours, revealing their every inner secret.

Good cop/bad cop techniques will be deployed against you. Make a request, any request, the negotiator will often say. Later, he will come back with the claim that he tried hard on your behalf "but we were turned down on that one." Notice the "we" as a point of common identification. It's an important concept. He's trying to get across the idea that you and he are "in this together."

The professional negotiator will use all of the information about you that had been previously gathered, couple it with whatever intelligence he can garner from his discussions with you, and do his best to keep you confused, dependent, and off balance. He will never talk to you in any manner that will allow a third party on the outside to hear what is going on. A member of the negotiating team will keep a giant running timeline listing all events, promises, actions, and requests in chronological order. As the siege wears on, they will go back to this material over and over in an attempt to demoralize and tire the retreaters.

Keep in mind that the main negotiator is charged with the duty of talking you into surrendering. He will lie like a Persian rug and promise absolutely anything to place you in custody, such as, "We don't really want to put you or your wife and kids in jail; come out peaceably and let's just get this ugly, uncomfortable situation behind us." No matter what federal negotiators promise, you will probably never see your wife and kids again if you turn yourself over to them!

Some experienced retreaters have suggested making tape recordings of all conversations with negotiators. Playing these back for people on the outside could produce dynamic results. It's probably not a bad idea to get copies of these tapes into the hands of your attorney on the outside or other sympathetic and responsible individuals who will know what to do with them.

As initially stressed, none of us can withstand the wiles of these professional negotiators. It's generally in your best interest not to talk to them at all. Instead, save precious time, breath, and thought for messages to the outside world. And then, don't attempt to harangue or propagandize whomever you reach. Simply stick to the facts of your case, bringing in as much compassion and humanity as possible. Play tapes of the federal negotiator's ploys as a contrast. Hopefully you will be able to raise serious questions among fellow citizens regarding the methods and motives of your tormentors.

Retreaters who find they must communicate with negotiators should always do so through some sort of third party filter. Negotiators despise this ploy because it effectively precludes them from using their charm, training, and experience to schmooze you into making concessions or admissions. Have all requests or questions put to this person and conveyed to you for consideration. It's a professional negotiator's worst nightmare.

GOING ON THE DEFENSIVE

Does this mean all is lost and that to retreat is a foolish, not even symbolically effective gesture?

Probably not. It means, first of all, that retreaters in our current society absolutely must keep their heads well down until government relaxes its control over our lives. Secondly, in spite of what has been conventional wisdom throughout the twentieth century, it is important to keep in mind that wars *can* be won by defensive actions. It doesn't always take the offensive kind to prevail. Generals don't want to believe it, but history is on our side on this one. Consider the following.

During the little known and mostly forgotten (except by the Finns) Winter War between the Soviet Union and Finland from November 30, 1939, till the armistice was signed on March 12, 1940, Finnish soldiers destroyed some 1,600 Russian main battle tanks and 900 combat aircraft and killed an estimated 200,000 Russian infantrymen. It was an epic contest between a nation of 4 million and one of 190 million. Finland didn't really destroy the Russian army; the Russian army hammering against stubborn Finnish resistance and horrible arctic weather destroyed itself.

Even the Germans, who directly caused millions of Russian casualties, couldn't accomplish the objective of destroying the Russian Army. And even though the Finns eventually "lost" militarily to the Russians, by fighting a wise defensive action on territory they knew very well, they effectively precluded what world leaders thought to be a quick, easy rape of a defenseless people.

Dozens of additional examples are out there, but one more is probably sufficient to get retreaters thinking about defensive actions as an overt, effective method of resistance. It is the battles of Kursk (or Citadel for German readers).

Kursk, as much as we Americans hate to admit, was the place where World War II was finally and decisively won for the Allies, and the Russians were the victors. It was and probably always will be the largest tank and infantry battle in world history. Yet many American history books fail to even mention the battle, even though it involved 2.2 million combatants, some 5,000 tanks, and well over 25,000 guns and mortars.

Russian officers at Kursk knew a German attack was likely. Rather than going on the offensive, however, they elected to dig in on four and even five levels of defense. Attacking Germans lost a certain percentage of their planes, tanks, and men at each line of defense until nothing was left with which to continue. Russian losses were large but not decisive or irreplaceable. Germany's losses at Kursk forever precluded it from controlling events on any front to the war's end in 1945.

HOLD OUT OR SURRENDER?

Many retreaters feel that the time is quickly approaching when the government will simply employ maximum force to wipe out any discovered retreats as quickly as possible. But like the survivors of the concentration camps of World War II, someone must live to tell the world what really happened so we can eventually bring these people to account.

So what to do if the government won't negotiate in good faith and prepares for a final onslaught? Retreaters then have the unfortunate choice of working to avoid death and destruction until the government gives up and goes away (unlikely), holding out as long as possible, or surrendering. Holding out is only practical if there is some hope of competing in the public relations portion of the defense. Those who surrender face months and probably years of illegal incarceration before charges are brought. Many simply disappear. Friends and family will have no idea where these people are being held or even if they are still alive. These prisoners will have all their property confiscated. Without a means to pay their attorneys, captured retreaters will find they are at the complete mercy of government officials. Most liken it to being held as a political hostage—a warning to others who might consider defying the government.

So hold out as long as you can and give up as dearly as possible. I sincerely hope I don't have to take my own advice some day, but I do know that every contemporary historian who has studied this situation agrees with Aleksandr Solzhenitsyn's assessment of the Stalin-era purges: "They could never have run over the top of us like they did if we had all resisted."

Chapter Nine

Government Weapons of Mass Destruction

If a retreat becomes seriously compromised and the situation deteriorates into a high-profile siege, you can be sure that government minions will deploy multimillion-dollar motorized weapons of mass destruction against you. Your odds of defending against such serious firepower can best be likened to putting in a McDonalds hamburger joint—the three most important considerations are location, location, and location.

Of course modern armored vehicles will eventually get through if their operators are determined to do so, but proper location makes it much, much more difficult and time consuming. Like defenders of the Warsaw ghetto, if you can make them take three months to do a job they figured would take three days, it can be considered a victory. However, it may be difficult explaining all of this to a dead wife and kids.

Given a choice between clever, effective concealment, therefore, and clever, effective use of barrier terrain—including swamps, creeks, rocky approaches, mine fields, and booby-traps—retreaters are best served choosing the former. Again, hiding rather than fighting is preferable for the modern retreater.

Even if retreaters are wildly successful at fending off or destroying weapons of mass destruction, government forces can always bring up one more bigger, better main battle tank,

*Other than making a brief political statement, retreaters can do little
against government weapons of mass destruction. Take out one or two
and there will always be more!*

helicopter, or armored personnel carrier. They can and will
eventually crush your retreat . . . but if they are unsure of your
location, they can't likely bring up the entire Eighth Panzers!

In any case, it is vital that all retreaters know their retreat
territory extremely well. Family members cannot be expected
to engage in military patrols or firefights, but if they know
every dip, swale, rock, and tree on the country they are
defending, they can slip in and out without undue danger.
This is one of the few successful counterstrategies that can be
employed to slip away to another retreat or organize a sapper
offensive against heavy enemy equipment.

Government agents will not stand by quietly while
retreaters destroy their heavy equipment, however. That fine
line between effective resistance and really upsetting one's
attackers is easily crossed. Should a retreat group succeed in
taking out a government APC, the deaths of crew members
may so infuriate authorities and the uninformed public that

your retreat will be summarily burned, blasted, bulldozed, and salted that very afternoon.

Those interested in the concepts in this chapter as well as many others related to dealing with attacking heavy equipment can read my book *David's Tool Chest* published by Loompanics Unlimited.

HELICOPTERS

Most helicopters are little more than flimsy flying aluminum cans surrounding some very delicate mechanisms. In the air or on the ground, it doesn't take much of a hit to do significant damage to most choppers. A single round, for instance, from an M1 carbine has successfully destroyed a HU-1B Huey. Furthermore, retreaters who choose locations amongst tall buildings, high mountains, or tall timber can mitigate the advantage attackers have from use of their choppers.

Helicopters used to attack and destroy retreaters can be roughly divided into three categories: strictly observation machines; lightly armored, lightly armed troop and weapons carriers; and heavily armed, hardened attack choppers.

Attack-type choppers such as Huey Cobras, Blackhawks, Hughes AH-6A4s, and Cheyennes are virtually impossible for retreaters to defend against. They are extensively armed and armored, fly very fast (close to 250 mph), and are extremely maneuverable. Calculating the proper lead and distance necessary to hit these targets is highly unlikely for laymen retreaters. They are even difficult to hurt while parked on the ground at the airport.

Having determined your exact location, attack chopper pilots can stand 600 to 1,000 yards beyond the reach of a citizen defender's weapons and, using sophisticated rockets and mini guns, chew almost any retreat to shreds in a few seconds. In fact, experienced pilots using modern aiming systems can consistently destroy targets no larger than a 55 gallon barrel at 1,000 yards. Best strategy when these machines show up is to quit the field to fight another day on more favorable terms.

Compromised retreaters may have to contend with three types of government helicopters: observation machines, weapon and troop transports, and serious assault choppers.

Fortunately for retreaters, there are few of these attack helicopters remaining in the world and even fewer experienced pilots to fly them. The end of the Cold War has produced a dramatic retrenchment in development and procurement of this class of machine. Meanwhile, normal attrition has cut their numbers, which, according to *The Illustrated Encyclopedia of Helicopters*, were never particularly large in the first place. As a result, retreaters are not likely to have to face hardened combat helicopters flown by experienced pilots.

In all likelihood, compromised retreaters will at least initially face police and municipal type observation choppers. Although they cannot return fire and will likely stand far, far off if fired upon, wise retreaters should not depreciate these light two-man observation crafts. Their pilots cannot risk having their machines holed even once by defenders, so they will always carefully stick to their original mission, which is observation. They will carry trained observers using 20-power gyrostabilized binoculars that can spot a single American ten cent piece at 1,000 yards. (I recently used a pair of these five-grand-each glasses on a spring black bear hunt. Only the word "insidious" can be used to describe them. We even identified birds 500 yards distance from a moving Jeep!)

Once located and identified, retreaters should expect to be harassed by standard, thin-skinned Huey type military choppers with mounted machine guns and armed troops in the doors. A single 7.62mm or 5.45mm round can penetrate these machines end to end and do material damage to relatively delicate flight controls, drive shafts, or transmissions. Although these choppers travel at speeds up to 125 mph, hitting them is difficult but not impossible.

Better yet, wise defenders will wait patiently until the machines are hovering at relatively short ranges. They may also try stringing heavy wire or light cable from tall trees in likely landing or pickup zones. Should pilots not see these lines, they can foul rotor control mechanisms, causing a sudden, violent crash. One such incident or even a near miss will really spook off other chopper pilots.

Helicopters often are not flown great distances from their pads to their targets. Government users initially may not even think about security when dealing with "crackpot" retreaters 15 miles away, leading to great opportunities for sniper or sapper attacks. Molotov cocktails or thermite grenades can decisively destroy even more sophisticated armed choppers. A single .30-caliber round fired into rotor hubs, fuel tanks, or transmissions will cause extensive damage, grounding machines for several days.

TANKS

Armed military personnel as well as VIPs from government agencies may ride to compromised retreat areas in helicopters, and there could be observation and possibly attacks from these machines, but the real on-the-ground threat will come from motorized armor of one sort or another.

The history of armor in combat is relatively recent. Incredibly, it is more recent than submarines or airplanes. The first use of tanks occurred on September 15, 1916, when 59 British tanks operated by eight-man crews charged out at the Germans on the Somme in northeastern France. Only nine of the original 59 completed the day's mission—all the others got stuck in the mud, broke down, or were holed or burned by the defending Germans.

The lessons learned that first day still work today. Tanks can be defeated by trapping them in unfavorable terrain, shooting holes in them, burning them, or simply waiting until they break down or run out of fuel.

Putting a hole in a tank still works nicely, but it requires a $60,000 wire-guided missile these days. Composition armor and depleted uranium plate afford protection about which early tankers could only fantasize. Even German machine gunners couldn't hole early British tanks, but they did pepper them with so many machine gun rounds that clouds of lead dust seeped in through riveted joints, jeopardizing the English crews.

Burning is another option, but it requires unusually large Molotov cocktails or thermite grenades placed inside the turret or engine component of the tank. As in times past, supporting infantry must be separated from the tank before attempting such a maneuver. Supporting infantry in a modern military tank context usually consists of helicopter-borne air-assault troops, and modern tank commanders are likely to request such helicopter troop support even in little actions against citizen retreats.

If you can somehow get close to enemy tanks, they are ideal candidates for surgically placed homemade thermite devices. Properly and wisely placed incendiaries will melt holes in the main gun, treads, drive mechanisms, transmissions, fuel cells, and even battery packs. Ruin one small part and the machine is out of service until the part is replaced or another machine is brought up.

Approximately 18 pounds of high-grade homemade explosive detonated firmly under a tank tread can cut the

If a tank shows up at your retreat there is little as a practical matter that can be done.

tread or break a drive sprocket, immobilizing the tank. A charge a third in size will immobilize even a large APC such as a Bradley, but retreaters setting out mines never know ahead what type of target will lumber along. Better too big than too small when it comes to immobilizing armor. Figure at least 40 pounds of high-grade homemade explosive under a tank to knock it out. Fully one barrel of much slower diesel-sensitized ammonium nitrate (about 750 pounds) is required to flip a modern tank on its back.

Military armor can be defeated by sudden, violent, adept deployment of commercial heavy construction equipment. Backhoes are able to dig trenches in which armor can be trapped, and a D-8 or D-9 Cat bulldozer can roll even an Abrams if deployed properly and with determination.

Always one of the great foils of any over-the-ground armor system is squishy or steep terrain. A knowledgeable U.S. Marine recently told me that most modern armor cannot operate properly on more than 50 percent of the American countryside for more than six months of the year. In many

The owner of this D-7 Caterpillar believes he can tip an Abrams tank over if he drives with aggression and skill.

cases during the winter and spring soft seasons, armor cannot get off established roads at all and cannot use many unpaved roads without becoming incapacitated.

Always keep in mind that 90 percent of a modern tank crew's time is spent outside their machine pulling maintenance. In-depth statistical analysis spanning 50 years of modern armored warfare proves that tank crews suffer a 25 percent casualty rate while outside their machines doing routine repairs. Retreat defenders who know their territory well can organize a sniper attack on offending armor and raise great consternation among exposed government forces. Similarly, because modern weapons of mass destruction require prodigious supplies of fuel and lubricants, fuel-hauling trucks are quick, easy pickings for defending snipers.

As of this writing it is difficult to believe that tank crews will actually discharge their main guns at fellow Americans, but if they do, keep in mind that these guns cannot reach down into below-level basements within cities at ranges of less than several hundred yards. Likewise, they are not designed to fire up past the third or fourth floor of a building unless the tank is several hundred yards distant. All tanks are completely blind to within about a 60 yard radius around them. Cause a tank crew to button up while it is separated from its support infantry and slowed down or stopped in rough terrain and it's a relatively easy matter to get up on it to deliver a Molotov. If the crew can see you, however, they can employ one of several light or heavy machine guns, which can reach up or down where the main gun cannot.

APCS

Modern Abrams tanks get about eight gallons of fuel to the mile. They cost more than $3 million each. As a result, most tinhorn dictators prefer to use cheaper, more common APCs against their populations. Armor-piercing rounds from .300 Winchester Magnum class rifles fired at relatively close range will pierce older APCs, but most Third World citizen defenders lack even this much armament. As a result, most of the world's citizens are at the mercy of these otherwise vulnerable machines.

A close friend of mine drove armored personnel carriers in Vietnam in the early days. Before the Vietcong or NVA had heavy weapons at their disposal, he simply drove around squashing the enemy in their foxholes This is about the same tactic used by government APCs trying to "take" a retreat. They drive round and round in ever narrowing circles until gradually all of the retreat's outside space is taken. By so doing, they test the depth of the defenders' resolve as well as determine what type of heavy weapons, mines, and traps the retreaters may have with which to deal with hostile armor.

It was common gallows humor among Vietnam-era APC drivers that .50-caliber rounds would not penetrate M-113s but "just tear in one side and bounce around inside," as one soldier told me. Since retreaters are much more likely to encounter APCs than main battle tanks (more than 60,000 American M-113 APCs in one configuration or another have been produced, not to mention scores of similar designs from other countries),

*Most retreaters have little effective defense against even modest govern-
ment armored vehicles such as this M-113 APC.*

they would be best served with .50-cal weapons such as Barrett
heavy sniping rifles to hole them with.

However keep in mind that it was land mines, not machine
guns or heavy rifle fire, that did in APCs in Vietnam. They got
as many as seven of our machines in one day, one GI told me.

Superficially, APCs are much like tanks. Their treads can
be blown off, they can be burned, they break down fre-
quently and require huge amounts of maintenance, and they
often get mired in bad country. Other differences, however,
are dramatic. In many cases sight distance out of modern
APCs is very good. When properly manned, it is very difficult to slip up on one. Over even terrain they are faster than
tanks, but on uneven ground they are extremely rough. At a
long ride's end, their passengers may be so shaken up they
will be unable to react properly. APCs lack trench and
water-hazard crossing capacity, but they can be airlifted into
remote areas. They definitely cannot bully their way
through heavy undergrowth, although some can swim
ashore from landing craft.

OTHER GOVERNMENT GEAR

Initially expect government minions to arrive at the retreat in regular civilian vehicles (if they don't arrive in high-handed fashion by chopper). Later, military vehicles such as 2 1/2 ton trucks and humvees will be deployed. All of these thin-skinned vehicles are subject to sniper fire, and all burn nicely when subjected to Molotovs or thermites placed carefully on motor blocks, transmissions, fuel cells, or amongst valuable cargo. Fire on tires is always dramatic.

Keep in mind that any hostage situation is very costly to governments. Burn a vehicle or destroy additional supplies and the bureaucrats will be at each other's throats about whose budget covers extra expenses.

Mortars and light, towable artillery are favored world over among those resisting tyrannical governments. Most portable artillery of this type comes captured from government forces. Iron of this sort is easily neutralized by sniper rifle fire or thermite, but in many cases the new owners would rather have it whole than in shot-up condition. I can't imagine that the U.S. government would deploy light artillery against a retreat, but who knows? These are strange times. Maybe some of us may even face ground attack jet aircraft, against which only quitting the field and hiding provides an effective answer.

It will probably depend entirely on to what extent we end up embarrassing or upsetting our rulers. Retreaters who wound or kill even a single government agent, even though they may be in the very act of murdering his wife or teenage daughter, can expect violent, irrational retribution. There can be no minimizing what will happen. "We cannot allow this heinous crime against authority to go unpunished," will be their war cry. Officials will attempt at all costs to ensure that only their version of the day's events is heard.

There is no question that intelligent, prepared retreaters could take out at least some government equipment in the event of an all-out assault. Doing so, however, will precipitate such a violent reaction that it is certainly not worth it in the end. So that leaves us with our original strategy: keep your head down, be obscure, don't let yourself become a target, and live till a better day. Retreating is about living. Let's do the best we can to stay alive.

Conclusion

There we have it.

Based on both historic and recent experience, we now know that our own government—not some invading foreign army or global nuclear war—is one of the greatest threats to individual freedom in the world today. We also realize that independent freedom-loving people may elect to retreat rather than submit to their agenda.

I may be wrong and am willing to be corrected, but it seems that every country in history has evolved into an assembly of common people who are plundered for the benefit of the elite ruling class. Given this fact of life, it is our continuing, everlasting duty to protect our private wealth, personal safety, care and nurturing of families and loved ones, and historic traditions from the grasp of increasingly despotic governments.

I do not wish to be trite, but three or four incidents of absolute devotion to cause in the face of a severe, unthinking, common enemy could cause a modern government to falter if the incidents are well publicized and public outrage sufficiently aroused. Like Valley Forge, it is terribly tough on those involved but terribly beneficial for those remaining outside.

Identifying exactly which part of government will constitute our greatest menace is and will always be our own personal responsibility. This probably won't be as difficult as it sounds since life's circumstances will throw all of us into touch with one portion of the bureaucracy or another. This will quickly identify those whom we must fear.

We also know how we can set up a retreat that can provide the necessities of life. In its simplest, most reduced form, requirements for life in a retreat—from an open, minimal family deployment across town to a deep retreat situated on terrain hostile to attackers—include nothing more than adequate food, water, and shelter. Planning ahead for these is not particularly difficult for average Americans.

Knowing when to leave for the retreat and how to get there in an emergency are vital issues. But now readers at least realize that they will have to address these issues.

Past experience demonstrates all too vividly that some very dedicated, well-trained, and well-equipped government agents will do their best to compromise any retreat that they see as a threat to their authority. Understanding ahead their means, methods, and devices provides a significant advantage to retreaters.

Citizen reluctance to downright unwillingness to submit to autocratic governments might put stress on and perhaps even reform such governments. Such types of defensive actions have won wars and changed societies. At the very least, issues once considered subversive or dangerous will cycle out with different regimes, allowing most retreaters to safely rejoin society after a few years.

Increasing personal technology, some believe, will allow freedom-loving people to more easily circumvent the iron grip on information held by dictatorial powers. Perhaps so. But experience suggests that governments have been brilliant at co-opting such technology for its own selfish ends.

For example, it used to be that free Americans could easily move their money around the world and start businesses without interference. Now computer archives, microfilm, and tremendously large data banks providing governments instant access to all manner of personal information regarding their citizens make this virtually impossible. Still, now that we know how little pieces of paper and errant computer files can provide an easy trail to our retreat, we can utilize modern technology to throw enough of our own paper out to cloud bureaucratic minds.

Historically, free minds and free spirits have been the fuel that fired successful economies. Unfortunately, bureaucrats will never understand the beneficial chaos created by freedom. Many officials don't care about human well-being just so long as everything is neat and in order. Joseph Stalin had maintenance men on the Moscow subway crew shot because they didn't keep trains on time—no matter that they couldn't because there were no repair parts!

But the lines on the graph may be crossing. More rules and regulations guarantee that more citizens will become targets of oppressive government officials. As a result, more citizens will find that they must retreat as a last resort in order to live peacefully and free. At the same time, there are demonstrably fewer free-minded people in our society. As the saying goes, animals born in the zoo do not understand freedom.

To be sure, most government officials will bad-mouth this information and the entire retreating philosophy. They will claim retreating is foolish, unnecessary, and unworkable. Only socially maladjusted, paranoid citizens will consider retreating, they will say.

I remind these officials that it was governments and governments alone that killed tens of millions of their own citizens in the twentieth century. At a minimum, Stalin had three separate KGB directors who each killed more citizens than Adolf Hitler, totaling about 40 million Russians (Hitler murdered 8 to 10 million). Mao is credited with about 50 million, and Pol Pot—that piker—could only do in about 3 million of his own citizens. And let's never forget government-sponsored genocides in Turkey, China, Guatemala, Uganda, and Rwanda.

But perhaps the U.S. government is sincere for once. Let's watch and see if it works to restrain itself so that retreat ideology and practice become unnecessary. Making retreats completely unnecessary, not statutorily illegal, would be the proof.

Nothing would please me more than to look back in 10 or so years to discover that our government actually did give up on bullying its citizens, that it admitted it can't stamp everyone into the same mold, and that average Americans did not end up needing retreat information to live free, peaceful, and productive lives.

Perhaps we retreaters—and freedom-loving people everywhere—can have an impact toward this end.